Transformational Leadership

Creating Organizations of Meaning

Also available from ASQ Quality Press:

The Trust Imperative: Performance Improvement through
Productive Relationships
Stephen Hacker and Marsha Willard

The Synergy of One: Creating High-Performing Sustainable
Organizations through Integrated Performance Leadership
Michael J. Dreikorn

The Change Agent's Guide to Radical Improvement
Ken Miller

Making Change Work: Practical Tools for Overcoming Human
Resistance to Change
Brien Palmer

The Executive Guide to Improvement and Change
G. Dennis Beecroft, Grace L. Duffy, John W. Moran

From Quality to Business Excellence: A Systems Approach
to Management
Charles Cobb

The Change Agents' Handbook: A Survival Guide for Quality
Improvement Champions
David W. Hutton

Strategic Navigation: A Systems Approach to Business Strategy
H. William Dettmer

From Baldrige to the Bottom Line: A Road Map for Organizational
Change and Improvement
David W. Hutton

Customer Centered Six Sigma: Linking Customers, Process
Improvement, and Financial Results
Earl Naumann and Steven H. Hoisington

To request a complimentary catalog of ASQ Quality Press publications,
call (800) 248-1946, or visit our bookstore at http://www.asq.org.

Transformational Leadership

Creating Organizations of Meaning

Stephen Hacker and
Tammy Roberts

ASQ Quality Press
Milwaukee, Wisconsin

American Society for Quality, Quality Press, Milwaukee 53203
© 2004 by ASQ
All rights reserved. Published 2003
Printed in the United States of America

12 11 10 09 08 07 06 05 04 03   5 4 3 2 1

Library of Congress Cataloging-in-Publication Data

Hacker, Stephen, 1955–
  Transformational leadership : creating organizations of meaning /
Stephen Hacker and Tammy Roberts.
    p. cm.
  Includes bibliographical references and index.
  ISBN 0-87389-610-6 (Hardcover, case bound : alk. paper)
    1. Leadership. 2. Organizational change. 3. Organizational
effectiveness. I. Roberts, Tammy, 1964– II. Title.

  HD57.7.H335 2003
  658.4'092—dc22   2003022147

Publisher: William A. Tony
Acquisitions Editor: Annemieke Hytinen
Project Editor: Paul O'Mara
Production Administrator: Barbara Mitrovic
Special Marketing Representative: David Luth

ASQ Mission: The American Society for Quality advances individual,
organizational, and community excellence worldwide through learning,
quality improvement, and knowledge exchange.

Attention Bookstores, Wholesalers, Schools, and Corporations: ASQ Quality
Press books, videotapes, audiotapes, and software are available at quantity
discounts with bulk purchases for business, educational, or instructional use.
For information, please contact ASQ Quality Press at 800-248-1946, or write to
ASQ Quality Press, P.O. Box 3005, Milwaukee, WI 53201-3005.

To place orders or to request a free copy of the ASQ Quality Press Publications
Catalog, including ASQ membership information, call 800-248-1946. Visit our
Web site at www.asq.org or http://qualitypress.asq.org.

 Printed on acid-free paper

Quality Press
600 N. Plankinton Avenue
Milwaukee, Wisconsin 53203
Call toll free 800-248-1946
Fax 414-272-1734
www.asq.org
http://qualitypress.asq.org
http://standardsgroup.asq.org
E-mail: authors@asq.org

AMERICAN SOCIETY
FOR QUALITY

To my family for their life-inspiring support—Marla, Jessica, and Mark.

To my husband Walt Roberts.

Table of Contents

Foreword

Today's leaders are in a turbulent situation. Some are considered remarkable, having put their organizations at the top. Others are considered evil, having led their organizations to disaster while growing richer without any consideration to their shareholders, to their employees, or to society. The same situation can be observed with political leaders as there is definitely a contrast between someone like Nelson Mandela and Slobodan Milosevic.

In his book *Good to Great*, Jim Collins shows that the most effective and successful organizations for the long term are those who have humble leaders not known by the media.

What makes the difference? What are the specific skills and behaviors that make a successful leader today?

Looking back to the middle of the 19th century, we see that the main characteristic of a leader was to be a good technician; he was asked to be a good financier, then a good salesman, then a good organizer, and so on. Over time, the role of leaders has changed because of the evolution of society and the economy. The leaders of tomorrow will not be the successful leaders of today. They will have all the skills of their predecessors plus something that will make the difference.

In this time of globalization and a world economy, there is a clash of different cultures. There is the western way, based on Greek philosophy, which focuses on effectiveness, targets, and objectives, and the Asian way of thinking, which focuses on opportunities and trends. Even *time* has different meaning: one uses *chronos,* with definite time and short-term objectives, and the other *keros,* meaning the right occasion, the right time to do something. Leaders all over the world have to cope with multiple cultures. Their decisions are based on different cultures and, therefore, lead to different effects.

Leaders stand at the edge of different fields. They stand between dreams and reality. They have to attract the energy to make the dreams last, and at the same time they have to cope with reality, which brings unexpected events.

They are judged on the results and not on their plans. They can have the best plan, but if an unexpected event leads to a failure, they will be judged on that.

How should a leader of the 21st century behave? They have to rely on past experience but, at the same time, enter into an unknown, new world where no solution is easy to find. They are alone with no reference to follow. They have to find skills and inspiration.

The end mission of a leader is to help individuals and organizations reach the essential goal. The essential goal is beyond our known world and beyond our control. It is inside us and not reachable. Over time, humans have tried to capture it in different forms of beliefs. It is through this ultimate goal that an organization will find its purpose and be in a position to bring its best to society and lead to success. Reaching the essential goal requires that you connect from the heart, explore with centeredness, balance and trust in the flow, and play with the rules, as in an infinite game.

To allow each individual and the organization to reach the essential goal, a leader has to bring spiritual and ethical values to the forefront, providing freedom and protection. They have to hold these values.

Society is moving, little by little, from the industry–commerce era to the creativity–communication era. We are entering into a new paradigm, and leaders will have a major role in helping themselves, the organization they are leading, and society reach this new step in the development of society.

We are entering into an era where an organization needs not only a leader at the top, but each individual within the organization will have to be a coleader. So the skills of new leaders have to be diverse. Everyone must lead in work, social life, and family.

I am delighted to see how this book addresses these different points in a very pragmatic way, allowing each person to find a way to transform self and the organization in which they are active for the success of the organization, the progress of society, and the happiness of all.

Bertrand Jouslin de Noray
Secretary General
European Organization for Quality

Acknowledgments

Marvin Washington for his enthusiasm and intellectual curiosity in the study of leadership.

The Performance Center Community as a source of creative organizational design and support.

Bertrand Jouslin de Noray for his explorative spirit and for his bold vision to build a community of transformational leaders who are awakened to their passion for quality and life, coming together in action to produce change across Europe.

Goaba Chiepe, Elias Magosi, Taboka Nkhwa, Norman Moleboge, Ikwa Bagopi, Eric Molale, Motsei Phiri, Olebile Gaborone, VT Seretse, Ruben Motswakae, and the many other friends in Botswana that have been a constant source of transformative inspiration.

Dick Gould for his backing of this project and the incredible leaders of the American Society for Quality Customer Supplier Division for their ongoing demonstration of a community in action.

Bob Dryden for his friendship and modeling of a positive life stance in the face of numerous obstacles.

Nelson King and our Bonneville Power Administration friends who work every day to discover how to better lead and manage a precious public asset.

Scott Sink for growing and maturing a world-class, action research center that provided fertile growing soil for the lively spirits found in The Performance Center Community.

Brad Wooten for sharing his ideas and knowledge on leadership and for his passionate commitment to transformation in higher education.

Pricilla Cuddy and Stephanie Holmes for adding to the transformation technology body of knowledge and moving state government to a new level of performance.

Karen Garst for her openness in sharing the transformational journey she is undergoing with her organization.

Doug Beigel for his passion and tenacity and for sharing his journey in creating an organization of meaning.

Mike Freese for being a transformational leader, doing the hard work, and actually having the measurable results to claim the accomplishment.

Steve Kroger for always standing by his principles and for his bold vision and results in transforming the quality of laboratory testing nationwide.

Larry Norvell, Jim Lussier, Greg Delwiche, and Jeanette Fish for enthusiastically sharing their personal insights in leading transformational change.

Bob King for his unique ability to translate knowledge into powerful tools that leaders can use to produce breakthrough results, and for his ongoing support and friendship.

Jeff Tryens for his work and experimentation in putting measurement systems to work in state government and for never tiring of sharing his expertise with the global community.

Sharon Flinder Conti for her advice and intellect in helping to shape the life planning tool.

Cindy Schilling, Marta Wilson, Altyn Clark, Ken Smith, Betty Cruise, and Tim Ludwig for being part of the crusade to discover the richness of organizational life.

Katie Marshall for her administrative contribution in pulling together this book.

My family—Mom, Dad, my sisters Dawn, Beth, Lisa, Tricia, and my brother Michael—for their love, for always standing by me, and for wanting the best for me.

Introduction

This book addresses the current revolutionary shift under way in the workplace and discusses the unique leadership required to produce organizational transformation. *Transformation* is the creation of discontinuous, step-function improvement in key result areas required for business success. Today, organizations exist in a rapidly changing global marketplace with increasingly complex customer requirements. As such, envisioning the need for transformational change is the primary directive of the leader and his or her top leadership team. With a view of the future in mind, the leader's job is to see how the organization must change, bringing focus to breakthrough strategies in key result areas. Whatever the requirements for radical change, the leadership team is charged with planning and leading others to produce essential transformation.

There are many great leadership books for the organizations of the '80s and '90s with subjects concerning change management, quality implementation, speed to market, market leadership, lean manufacturing, creation of high-performance work systems, and so on. However, each of these texts misses a focus on the dynamic shift in the workplace. The incremental change and standardization skills espoused in these texts are still necessary, but the role of transformational leadership has become a growing requirement for success.

Transformational leadership means the comprehensive and integrated leadership characteristics required of individuals, groups, or organizations traveling the road to transformation. Integral to transformational leadership is the ability of the leader to bring clarity of purpose and meaning into the organization. Creating places of purpose, once thought a New Age fad, is now a survival card for organizations as competent workers increasingly seek out meaning in their work and rapid changes in the market necessitate transformational change. So, as leaders, how do you create a place where purpose dominates action and where individual spirit radiates?

Many leadership frameworks include trait and behavioral models in which the determination of a successful leader is seen in the characteristics and actions of an individual. Additionally, the concept of situational leadership gives recognition of a leader's need to adapt to a variety of conditions and environmental factors, thus the step of making a determination of leadership opportunity prior to engaging a particular skill or approach. In 1983, the competing values framework was introduced by R. E. Quinn and J. Rohrbaugh, stressing the need for leaders to have a broad pallete of skills to tackle the four stages of a new organization. The stages form polar opposites, thus requiring a leader to be versatile.

The transformational leadership model introduced in this text explores a particular aspect of leadership—the leadership required to achieve a step-function change in results. First, we discuss consciousness of the leader, relationships, and the enterprise. Then paralleling these perspectives, the leadership requirements are broken down into self-mastery, interpersonal mastery, and enterprise mastery. Furthermore, we paint the situational requirements of such radical change with the essential leadership responses in terms of skills and behaviors. Complementary texts could easily include the best manner to bring an organization into control or ways to establish a continuous improvement culture. But what is illustrated in this book is the leadership required for transformational change, the kind of change that is part of long-term, successful organizations.

These ideas, however, cannot by themselves create transformational leaders. Just learning to articulate these principles and models guarantees nothing in terms of actual leadership skills. Warren Bennis is a prolific writer and an enormous contributor to the understanding of leadership in today's time. And some time ago he put forth this warning:

> There is no simple formula, no rigorous science, nor cookbook that leads inexorably to successful leadership. Instead, it is a deeply human process, full of trial and error, victories and defeats, timing and happenstance, intuition and insight. Learning to be a leader is somewhat like learning to be a parent or a lover, your childhood and adolescence provide you with basic values and role models. Books can help you understand what's going on, but for those who are ready most of the learning takes place during the experiment itself.[1]

We address transformational leadership pulling from our collective leadership and consulting experience, current thought leaders, successful transformational leaders, and a growing body of knowledge including original research. The concepts and experiences captured here are but a guide in becoming a transformational leader. The work you are considering or are currently engaged in will be the developmental ground for the actual skills of transformational leadership.

We present stories of transformational leaders from a variety of organizations and leadership positions. These leaders have created the requisite step-function improvement results within their own organizations. Their perspectives are rich with advice from a self-reflective viewpoint.

So we launch into the topic of transformational leadership with eyes wide open and a hunger for discovering the requirements for inducing radical improvement. We welcome you along.

ENDNOTE

1. Warren Bennis and Burt Nanus, *Leaders: The Strategies for Taking Charge* (New York: Harper & Row, 1985): 223.

1

What Is Transformation?

Transform, from the Latin word *transformare*, means to "change the nature, function, or condition of, to convert."[1] And the concept of transformation can be applied to various entities: relationships, individuals, groups, teams, communities, or political systems. If organizational transformation is sought, it is defined by marked change in the nature or function of the systems and subsystems that comprise the organization. To be more precise, when transformation is viewed from a creation standpoint, not as an unexpected occurrence, organizational transformation takes on the added descriptor of the results created. Distinctly positive results are normally sought. Therefore, the complete definition of *organizational transformation* becomes *the marked change in the nature or function of organizational systems creating discontinuous, step-function improvement in sought-after result areas.*

This definition requires both the discernment of the changes generating the transformation and the ensuing performance results. The results are a consequence of the system changes. And the results are of a certain character. Change can take on many different patterns in terms of scale and importance. A basic but powerful change is standardization, or a reduction in variation. Standardization involves decreasing variation in how a system performs. The results of standardization are a more predictable system. A majority of people within an organization is focused upon the operating systems, and can find ample opportunities to *tighten* the execution of systems and deliver a reduction of variation in performance. By contrast, continuous improvement efforts are aimed at achieving gradual, positive changes in performance. In a statistical sense, standardization is about reducing variation, while improvement is about shifting the mean.

Differing from reduction of variation or continuous improvement, step-function improvement constitutes a dramatic and pointed shift in results. Also referred to as *breakthrough improvement,* its hallmark is a conspicuous shift in results. It can be seen on a control chart as a discontinuous break with past results, a step up in performance, breaking from the previous system results. For transformation to be declared, the results are categorized as step-function or breakthrough improvement. This is important because one cannot declare a transformation without the measurable results to demonstrate the change. A transformation in thinking is not hidden. Transformed thinking produces resulting actions and altered actions create changed results.

Obviously, the nature and pattern of previous system results help determine what qualifies as a leap in results. To avoid an endless conversation about the magnitude of results, Figure 1.1 demonstrates the profile of charted results in each of the three categories previously mentioned.

In some cases, what is measured and the metric used to denote improvement shifts its focus due to transformation. For instance, if one is measuring dissatisfaction with a product or service as the current understanding of quality, an organization may measure customer complaints as its sole metric. But with a new light and focus on the customer's experience and desire to create customer delight, customer satisfaction could be the fresh perspective and customer testimonials the metric in focus. A step-function drop in customer complaints will be experienced, but the focus on taking actions to achieve customer satisfaction will produce breakthrough results as measured by testimonials. The object to measure has shifted.

Transformation occurs within the organizational systems and subsystems (nested systems). These systems are brought into being, sustained, and guided by leaders. Consequently, for the organization to undertake radical change, the leaders must be suited to create the desired transformation.

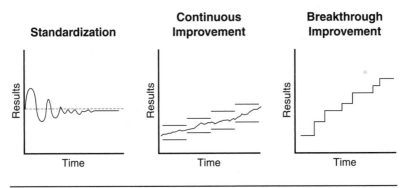

Figure 1.1   Performance curves for standardization, continuous improvement, and breakthrough improvement.

The study of transformational leadership is, therefore, brought to the surface. The study is an examination of what constitutes leading a marked change in organizational systems, resulting in step-function improvement in sought-after results. Transformational leadership is *the comprehensive and integrated leadership capacities required of individuals, groups, or organizations to produce transformation as evidenced by step-functional improvement.*

An approach to transformational leadership is the topic at hand. This leadership approach, in particular, was designed to be integrated and holistic, serving as a powerful framework to anchor your own ideas and experiments in leadership. Without this kind of comprehensive framework, leaders are at risk of continually adopting the latest leadership style-of-the-day found in the local airport bookstore. While new approaches can be insightful, holding a comprehensive, integrated view of leadership gives you a Christmas tree, so to speak, on which to hang the latest ornament.

Through our leadership readings and experiences in working with organizations to produce transformation, we have discerned that a new kind of leadership is required. At the heart of transformational leadership is a consciousness within the self and the ability to raise consciousness in others. The required skills are both managerial and leadership, not one over the other, and knowing when to call upon a specific skill in a given situation. Figure 1.2 represents the world of transformational leadership. The next

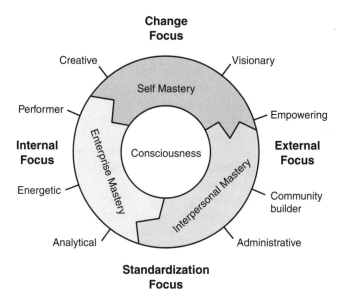

Figure 1.2 Transformational leadership model.

several chapters present a more detailed look at each component of the model, breaking it down into pieces to better convey the depth of ideas embodied in the approach.

To begin our study of transformational leadership, we explore three perspectives: the leader as an individual, interpersonal relationships, and the organization as a whole. Consider each perspective a prospect for transformation. The individual leader is at the core of the change, and the change may have to be initiated at the core of the leader. Inside, the leader may require transformative change to exert the essential leadership in a rapidly altering environment. Personal transformation is then a subject to be investigated. Likewise, relationships form entities in and of themselves, and a step-function improvement in relationship results can provide the transformative energy needed to shift the results of the entire organization. Finally, the organization composed of its systems, including relational systems, offers a target for transformation. So, to adequately address organizational transformation, the perspectives of individual leaders, relationships, and the organization as a whole must be considered when contemplating transformation.

PERSONAL TRANSFORMATION

Forming the foundation of any organization are individuals—individuals who have learned a successful way to behave and act within the organization. To be in a position of influence within the organization, traditional leaders represent role models of how to think, respond, and perform the business of the organization. Their reward has been a move into levels of higher responsibility. Normally, the responsibility entails holding the organization, group, and/or team within a set of practices and methodologies that has produced some level of past success. But there is the problem. The requirements for the organization to be successful in the future may well be quite different from the present requirements. Therefore, an individual transformation often becomes a prequisite for the transformation of the organization. A personal rebirth into a perspective of possibilities, not a step-by-step managerial formula, is required.

For example, Peter moves up rapidly within the sales and marketing functions of his product division. Focusing upon a mentor within the company's hierarchy, he does well by imitating the style and methods of a successful leader. To his credit, he works hard, learns fast, and is promoted to head of the division. But in times of dramatic market shifts, his tried and true methods falter. Frustrated when the processes utilized in the past fail to deliver, Peter seeks to find deficiencies within his employees. After dismissing a number of his employees and alienating the majority of the remaining ones, he finds himself no closer to turning around the downward performance of his new division. His leadership was based upon techniques, not principles that were easily adaptable to new conditions. He looks to his mentor to supply the answers. However, the advice of his mentor appears to be too general and too broad for Peter to use in his new role as division head. What Peter wants to know are the exact actions he should take to alleviate the current problems and create success within his division.

Now, it could be sad news for Peter, but it also could be the start of a personal transformation. The opportunity to transform is often found in the moment of crisis, for example, with the failure of old behavior patterns to yield results. Imagine Peter on a wooden platform that is ablaze with the fires of problems and poor results. This burning platform appears to be manageable, at first, if he puts some attention to the edges where crisis fires have broken out. However, as the flames roar up and the fire takes the upper hand, he is faced with choices. Peter can either deny that the fire is threatening (the results really aren't that bad) and focus on those he believes responsible for the fire—or move off the platform to a new future. The burning platform could form the impetus to change, to transform his thinking and approach. A personal crisis of leadership could result in a real look at his dependence on methodologies and help him construct new leadership principles based upon a transformed view of himself and his effectiveness.

Burning platforms can take many forms—broken marriages, consequences of unhealthy physical or psychological practices, or near death experiences. The shock of failure, when seen with a causal mind-set, can start a rebirthing process. By causal mind-set, we refer to the ownership of the failure by the person and not the shifting of blame to others. When Peter recognizes his connection to the unacceptable results of the division, the division he leads, the door opens for transformation. Many leaders never achieve this understanding and consistently claim success as their sole creation but their failures as the product of others.

There are other beginnings to personal transformation. In *The Conscious Manager: Zen for Decision Makers*, Fred Philips calls out the power of an *opening experience* to develop consciousness:

> Opening experience—a moment of meditation, a work of art, a waterfall or sunset, or a passing experience of selfless flow in an athletic or job-related teamwork. Any of these can lead to the realization, "Why, yes, there is more to life than I thought." This is not always a transformative experience: it may be quite fleeting. But it is a brief glimpse into the oneness of things, a reassuring moment without ego.[2]

This realization may shed some light on possible beginnings of personal transformation, but the heart of personal transformation lies within a newfound consciousness. For many people, going through the daily motions becomes a substitute for exploration. Excitement of discovery and self-discovery has been replaced by tedious routines and reinforced views of life itself established deep in the hard drives of the mind. The transformation nucleus is a questioning of self and an awareness of self. It exists in an ongoing dialog with the self and opens up the possibility for radical change. As David Bohm and Mark Edwards explain:

> At this point, we can say that whenever something happens that causes people to question their thought seriously, for that moment they are beginning to awaken perception. They're not just running the disks automatically. Up till now the disks ran automatically, producing the answers that would make people feel better.
>
> Coming back to this matter of questions, a window of opportunity has opened up, and if we don't take advantage of it, it will close—these questions don't stay open indefinitely. Gradually the disks adapt to close the window. There is a constant tendency in thought to prevent questioning, to prevent this sort of thing from being opened up for inspection, because it might be disturbing. So the longer we wait, the greater chance there is for this self-deception process to work, unless we fairly quickly do something that is really to the point.[3]

Awakening to a newfound consciousness is the central aspect of personal transformation. So in building a transformational model, we start with consciousness at the central point (Figure 1.3). This placement implies that the core feature of transformation is a consciousness of self. Understanding one's life purpose, observing the self from an objective as well as from a subjective viewpoint, engaging in dialog with the self and seeing the self in relationship to a larger life spirit are all aspects of consciousness.

RELATIONAL TRANSFORMATION

It would simplify matters greatly if transformation was left to the sole domain of personal transformation. But a defining characteristic of an organization is one of interpersonal relationships. Thus, reality dictates that relationships become a focus of organizational performance. Stronger relationships build stronger teams, which fosters stronger team-to-team dynamics and ultimately a stronger, more robust organization.

Figure 1.3   Personal transformation and consciousness.

As with personal transformation, relational transformation begins with consciousness. It is the consciousness of the relation itself that is sought in this case—not just having two conscious individuals in a relationship. The relationship itself is an entity. And the consciousness questions revolve around the relationship's direction, purpose for being, and results produced. A conscious relationship is one that exists for a purpose: possibly to create a household for child rearing, friendship, a vocational vision, sport, or a host of multiple reasons. Furthermore, such relationships have direction and mindful history. The uniqueness of the relationship is cognizant, with an awareness of its workings.

Conversely, an unconscious relationship is seen when the reason for the relationship is explained simply because it has been that way, or the parties view themselves as being thrown together and wandering through life in the same space. Maybe there exists a codependency, but neither party is attentive to its true meaning. As a result, transformation is difficult at best because the parties are not alert *from what to what.* This is not to say that unconscious relations are bad or even dysfunctional, but they lack power and are not as productive as when the relationship has purpose and direction.

For the organization, having conscious relationships with purpose and direction creates a fruitful environment in which to introduce radical change. The relationships are more resilient and can better handle turmoil brought

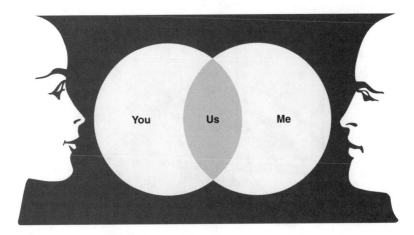

Figure 1.4   Relational transformation and consciousness.

about from the surroundings. Relationships with a high level of awareness are better able to transform themselves and produce more value within the relationship. Sometimes this is referred to as deepening a relationship.

Indeed, for a relationship to transform, consciousness is also required (see Figure 1.4). Consciousness of the individuals in the relationship may be a stepping-stone, but it is inadequate in achieving high-performance relationships. The special chemistry within a relationship is often the product of purposeful creation. It is a creation that goes beyond self-service to serving the relationship.

ENTERPRISE TRANSFORMATION

The enterprise, the undertaking itself, requires consciousness if, indeed, the organization is to transform. There is a subtle distinction between enterprise and organization. The concept of *organization* is *the various functions and elements that form an entity*—an organism, as it would be. Individuals, groups of persons, processes, assets, and other elements compose the organization. *Enterprise* is *the endeavor, the purpose being pursued, and the methods employed.* Consciousness of the enterprise points to people's degree of awareness of a particular endeavor and their collective understanding of its scope, risks, and intricacies.

So, when speaking of transforming the enterprise, the reference is to transforming the undertaking, the conceptual aspect of the endeavor. A transformation of the enterprise might look like a shifting toward the pursuit of sustainable business growth versus market expansion. Transformation of the enterprise might be from fundraising for a cause to a focus on the cause with fundraising seen as but one method.

Look at the family enterprise. The family is an organization with an infrastructure, planning methods, motivational systems, communications, and so on. But what is the enterprise? What does the family exist for? Is it to nurture children, provide for safety, afford emotional support, grant a safe haven for restoration, or some of all the previous purposes? Of importance is the collective consciousness of all family members to a purpose, whatever it is. To the extent the family entity has a collective consciousness toward a reason for being, the more productive the family will be in achieving its end. A transformation of the family enterprise might be a shift from some people who live in the same house and occasionally eat together to a unit that provides emotional support and a learning environment for all members. The results would look different given the shift in focus—thus a transformation of the enterprise.

CONSCIOUSNESS

A level of appreciation in leading transformation may be growing. The difficulty is in the need to have individuals, especially the leader, be transformative in nature, to have relationships jump to a high productive stance, and the enterprise itself to have breakthrough improvement (see Figure 1.5).

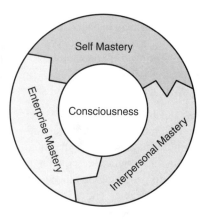

Figure 1.5 Transformational perspective ring.

And at the heart of each transformational perspective, consciousness is found. An awareness of self by the leader, of relationship entities, and of the enterprise all constitute a sensitivity to something greater than programmed responses based upon fear of past experiences alone. Amplifying consciousness in people's daily lives is not an easy undertaking. As such, we offer a framework that considers consciousness from three points of view: *consciousness of purpose, consciousness in the moment,* and *consciousness of the greater.*

Consciousness of purpose applies to self, relationships, and the enterprise. Are you conscious of your own life's purpose? Is the relationship conscious of its unique purpose? Do the people who make up the enterprise hold a collective consciousness of the organization's endeavor?

Consciousness in the moment is the observer-self. Can you observe your own mind-set in the moment and see how it is adding positively or negatively? Can you have a conversation with another person about yourself, being casual in sharing how your own thinking hinders your relationship? Is the entity conscious in the moment? Can you hear what your customers are saying in the moment, or are you caught in a past story about your customer's needs?

Consciousness of the greater requires an awakening beyond self-interest: a connection to something greater than the relationship, the enterprise, or ourselves. How does my life's purpose serve the greater good? How does an expression of love in a marriage serve the community? How is an organization contributing to the community in which it resides?

The unconscious mind simply chooses to remain asleep to the greater possibilities open to all, asleep to the magnificent creative powers bestowed upon each one person. And it is a choice everyone has the responsibility to make as individuals. Conscious and engaged, or asleep and reactive are the choices at each minute of a person's life. And if you choose consciousness, then even larger challenges await in consciousness of relationship entities and collective consciousness of the enterprise.

In his book *Flow,* Mihaly Csikszentmihalyi states the following:

> To develop selves capable of dealing with the evolutionary forces rushing us to the third millennium, it is imperative to become better acquainted with the functioning of the mind. You can drive a car all your life without knowing how the engine works, because the goal of driving is to get from one place to the next, regardless of how it is done. But to live an entire life without understanding how we think, why we feel what we feel, what directs our actions is to miss what is most important in life, which is the quality of

experience itself. What ultimately counts most for each person is what happens in consciousness . . .

What are you making happen consciously—in your self, in your relationships, and in your organization? Consider this your call to consciousness. Are you investigating how your thoughts are being constructed, or are they on autopilot and relying upon reactive schemes? Consider this a wake-up call, a call to consciousness in all you do. This consciousness will be the basis for a new understanding of how you create the world around you. And it will serve as a basis for transforming to something much more powerful and meaningful. Let's explore why unique leadership is required to transform organizations.

At the end of each chapter, key lessons are summarized for review and discussion with other leaders within your organization.

SUMMARY LEARNINGS

1. *Transformation* is defined as *the marked change in the nature or function of organizational systems creating discontinuous, step-function improvement in sought-after result areas.*

2. *Transformational leadership* is defined as *the comprehensive and integrated leadership capacities required of individuals, groups, or organizations to produce transformation as evidenced by step-functional improvement.*

3. Continuous improvement and standardization are valuable to individuals and organizations but alone are insufficient in today's changing world.

4. Three perspectives are valuable in understanding organizational transformation: personal, relational, and enterprise.

5. Consciousness is essential in the transformation process—consciousness of self, of relational entities, and of the body enterprise.

Each chapter of this book offers suggestions for turning these ideas into action. We recommend that you take time at the end of each chapter, or after you have completed the book, to reflect on the questions presented. The questions are designed to raise your consciousness as a transformational leader, to reinforce the key ideas and concepts in each chapter, and to offer ways of translating your acquired knowledge into meaningful, practical action.

TO ACTION

1. What are some past step-functional improvements or breakthrough results you have created in yourself? What prompted the transformation?

2. What are some past step-function improvements or breakthrough results you have created in relationship with others? What prompted the transformation?

3. What are some past step-functional improvements or breakthrough results you have created in your organization?

4. How can you categorize your current change efforts designed to shift performance results within your organization into transformational (breakthrough), continuous improvement (incremental), and standardization (reduction of variation)?

ENDNOTES

1. *The American Heritage Dictionary of the English Language,* Fourth Edition (Boston: Houghton Mifflin, 2000).
2. Fred Philips, *The Conscious Manager: Zen for Decision Makers* (Beaverton, OR: General Informatics, 2003): 118.
3. David Bohm and Mark Edwards, *Changing Consciousness* (San Francisco: Harper, 1991): 32.

LEADERSHIP VIGNETTE

Mr. Jim Lussier

Leadership Position: CEO

Organization: St. Charles Medical System, Bend, Oregon

Transformational Results: In 1989, Jim Lussier set out to transform St. Charles Medical Center (SCMC). Jim's vision and breakthrough results have captivated people around the world, causing many to question existing paradigms. The breakthrough results of lower costs, reduced length of stay, higher patient satisfaction, award-winning service and a waiting list of nurses desiring employment, all demonstrate the skills of leading transformation and building an organization of meaning.

SCMC breathes new life into the possibility that authentic caring can return to a medical system, which for many patients and their families is currently sterile and heartless. And for many doctors, nurses, and other caregivers, the medical systems in which they exercise their vocations are frequently places where spirit is thwarted. SCMC, under Jim's leadership, has created something quite different from the norm in healthcare services. To design and successfully implement his vision for holistic and integrated care, Jim employed over 250 task forces to look at how existing care processes and hospital procedures must change to better serve patients. Through this five-year effort, Jim and his staff redefined healthcare delivery by recognizing that the spirit of love and compassion must be partnered with technology and intellect in healing the body. Every process and hospital procedure was reengineered, and the staff was trained in a patient-relationship-centered approach to care. Innovation and experimentation was encouraged among the staff, and creativity continues to flourish.

Reflections on Transformation[1]

How did you build your vision and involve others in it?

I set out to create a new vision of the organization. On a personal level, I was clear in my own mind that we were not just in the business of fixing people. Our job is to create a continuum of services to *potentiate* health. Hospitals can be extremely spiritual in their orientation. We don't want employees that are there just to make a few dollars. We want to attract employees that have a mission in life to help others. This is extremely important. Improving the health of those we serve in the spirit of love and compassion was the most significant conversation that the board has undergone. To be held accountable at that level is both bold and daunting. However, we now take joy in the wonderful opportunity to tell the world that this is what we strive for.

What has the role of your organizational values played in the transformation of SCMC?

We place a high value on the importance of human relationships. This includes the relationship with our patients, families, friends and also our relationship with one another. We want to be perceived as a place that cares for people. We have to be about the relationship and the business in order to be successful. SCMC has to be a human place, a place that appreciates human values. If we can't heal each other, then we can't provide that for our patients.

What were some of the strengths of your teams?

We intentionally moved away from hierarchy in organizing the transformation effort and utilized empowered teams to guide the change that needed to happen. Today, we employ very few reporting relationships. Our clusters of teams get the daily work done. Most bosses are actually team leaders. We have a leadership council that is delegated responsibility for daily operations with an executive staff that sets the parameters. Then, we turn it over to the leadership team and work teams to execute. Our managers used to spend a lot of time solving problems between employees. However, because we have trained folks on patient-centered teams, they solve their own problems. Each team forms *interactive agreements* and are given the opportunity to determine how they are going to work together. Anytime an agreement is violated, we let one another know. This level of openness, directness, and accountability reduces conflicts and builds trust.

How do you respond to the changing world?

The world is changing so fast, changing from one paradigm to another. It is the obligation of the leader to be a futurist. My concept of the future is that it doesn't exist. Our job as leaders is to see the future as a void to be created and we're the designers. We become the interpreters of the future. I have set a goal to read 52 books a year, one a week, to expand my view of the world. I strive to respond to the changing world including rapidly changing technologies and new patient needs. We have also expanded our mission. The work we do is not just about providing care in Bend, Oregon. We now operate in a global market with the opportunity to care for people in Europe and around the world. In addition, we see our competition not simply as other healthcare providers. Our competition is Land's End, Toyota, Federal Express, Nordstrom, and Ritz Carlton because they are redefining customer service. Naturally our patients will compare their experience with us to these standard setters. What's happening in the world both within and outside healthcare is becoming really important. Personal empowerment is also becoming very important, and this has huge implications for our organization. Generation X'ers are totally different in terms of their needs and wants. Unfortunately, we have a bias in healthcare that we won't do anything unless it's reimbursed. The problem with this limited view of the environment in which we operate is that we fail to see opportunities all the time. We need to build different organizations. We can learn a lot from other industries that have been through similar change.

What contributed to the success of this change initiative?

It is extremely important to understand how we design organizations. Big, bureaucratic organizations are being left in the dust. They can't keep up with the rapidly changing world. Dee Hock's work on the formation of worldwide, flat, networked organizations using technologies and organized around guiding principles allows organizations to be flexible, which is imperative in today's changing world.

I have learned that change takes a long time. Continue to persevere. Always back off to give people some room to adapt, but never back down from the goal. There are a whole variety of ways to reduce the resistance to change. Use them and experiment. My organization has a whole department focused on reducing resistance. In today's world, you will always have to manage change.

What words of wisdom can you share with others embarking on the road to transformation?

Create a foundation for success and a focused vision shared by all. Set bold and audacious goals. In healthcare, people get really turned on by taking care of the comprehensive needs of the patients. Be a synergistic organization. Differentiate and characterize services, defining who you want to be, and provide value-added services. Continue to look at where you want to go. Fail faster and try new things. The world need not be win/lose; it can be win/win. Competition is way overrated. We have spent many, many resources competing against one another. When you play the game of win/lose, you are always the smallest fish.

ENDNOTE

1. Transcript excerpts, interview with Jim Lussier, June 13, 2003, Portland, Oregon, conducted by Tammy Roberts.

2

Why Transform?

Do not hold the false impressions that transformation is inherently good, that it possesses an intrinsic worth, or that the transformational journey merits traveling for the experience itself. Transformation is embarked upon for the single reason of improving results—and doing so drastically. Transformation of the leader and the organization is a tough undertaking. It requires a remaking of individual skill sets and radical change within an organization. Some people choose not to set upon such a course. Some leaders choose not to take their organizations through the knothole of transformation.

There are many societal segments crying out for an abrupt change in results, in dire straits due to outdated processes and approaches. But this does not mean that the sitting leadership will lead transformational change. It is an option, at least in the short term, for leaders to delay radical change. Often the appearance of change is demonstrated by in-vogue organizational development-speak and motivational posters on every wall. "Why transform?" can be answered not only in the need for transformation but as a rhetorical question with personal risk in mind.

Primary and secondary education is an example of a societal area in need of transformation. Increasingly deluged with new challenges and unmet expectations, educational reform appears to be a constant cry. And indeed, many exemplary leaders have taken these challenges head on. But often, performance appears to be captured in pronouncements of learning excellence rather than concrete actions and measured success. School principals are being asked to move forward with radical change in order to develop inspired students instead of providing holding pens where the desire for lifelong learning is squelched. Elaine L. Wilmore and Cornell

17

Thomas express the need for transformational change and the type of leader required:

> Today's schools face an array of problems that administrators in the past did not have to address. Besides societal issues, there are important policy and regulatory issues such as the future and effect of school privatization, vouchers, and charter schools. No one can say exactly where such proposals will lead. But one thing is for certain. We cannot keep managing schools as if they are independent entities unconnected to the community as a whole. To produce the results necessary, a transformational leader is required to march student and teacher, academically and personally, into the new century with a love and desire for future learning. Anything less we cannot afford. A transformational leader seeks to change schools as we have known them into caring, responsible, knowledge rich, competent, change-oriented centers of the community. These schools are places where all students truly can and will learn.[1]

The separation of those principals rising to the test and those choosing to sit back and hope for a miracle is becoming evident. Like many segments of our society, the demand for results is causing a shakeout, a separation of leaders. Wilmore and Thomas speak directly to school principals and their choice of leadership:

> Real leaders are never satisfied with the status quo. They are always seeking to change, to improve, and to reflect on "How can I do this better next time?" There is always a next time. "Wannabe" leaders are afraid of failure. In truth, they are afraid of change. They would rather stick with what they have, because they at least know what it is—a primary reason so many schools are low performing. Such principals have no vision of excellence, regardless of circumstance, because they have let fear overrule the need for change. Without a specific vision of excellence, how can anyone be expected to inspire greatness in others? How can anyone sell a dream, a vision, or a plan that has not been worked out and committed to in his or her own mind?[2]

Our schools are not alone in the onslaught of new requirements and challenges. Nor are they in quarantine, with an unacceptable percentage of their leaders stricken with the illnesses of unpreparedness, fear, and inaction. Why have leaders en masse not risen to provide the direction for transforming organizations, communities, and relationships?

It is because leaders are making different choices: some seize the opportunity for change while others do not. The excitement of creation and step-function improvement has grabbed many leaders, bolstering their energies and accelerating their results. "Why transform?" as seen through these eyes is energy inducing, the right journey for the leader and the organization—a way of life. Others hope they can make it to retirement or simply survive the fallout. In the short term, leaders actually have the option not to transform, given the slow movement of the average organization to address leadership behaviors or results. This is both in praise and in negative job action. Organizations move at glacial speed in part because transformation itself seems to be an option. The unspoken questions are, I am working as hard as possible, isn't this enough? Why the risk? Why transform?

KEY PRESSURES

But seeing transformation as optional does not mean the world stands still and accepts the previous performance levels. In today's world, turning up the work output rheostat is insufficient. What is required is a remaking, a reconsideration of the organization. In the past, a major rethinking of the organization was mandatory every decade or so for survival. Needless to say, the world is turning at a faster pace. Three key pressures calling for increased performance through transformation are an increase in societal complexity, increased competition, and shifting technology and social standards.

Increase in Societal Complexity

As our societal systems reach higher levels of interdependency, the interlocking nature of daily life strains both the individual and the organization. Think about losing your wallet. Fifty years ago, the loss of your wallet would mean a loss of cash. Sad, but not tragic. But in today's world, the loss of the cash would be the least of your concerns. Your credit cards, debit card, driver's license, and insurance identification would all have to be replaced. Not an easy task given the interactions with large systems all having differing requirements. And identity theft adds a whole new level of concern. The complication to replacing the items in your wallet was created as hurdles were put into place to solve other problems, but in turn created new problems.

In the book *Changing Consciousness*, David Bohm and Mark Edwards state, "We keep coming back to this point that complex technology requires the exercise of greater intelligence—a different way of thinking—if each new development is not to create more problems."[3] This is a different way of thinking and a different way of approaching change. The leadership lessons of the present are derived in large part from the past. Even if it is the recent past, rapid change has rendered many of these lessons obsolete.

A base teaching involves separating personal life from business and professional life. This approach may have had validity in its time but not today. Many organizations have recognized the complexity of daily living and have responded with on-site services ranging from banking to daycare. Not long ago, having on-site food service was considered a blessing. Organizations are much more considerate of support services for employees, seeking ways to make living easier by integrating more of life with work.

Increased Competition

What was once seen as great performance locally is now viewed from a global perspective, a global comparison. The result is that great local performance is often average when seen through a global set of glasses. The world is shrinking because of both global communication and an increase in population. As a result, performance expectations have increased.

It is not only competition for goods and materials. The competition is around ideas and the idea generators. One large electronics business, which we have worked with, finds it competitive to secure engineering support in Israel and India, manufacturing in Germany and England, and enhanced assembly in the United States. This example is not uncommon, but the leadership skills required with such an international team, especially in a technical field, calls upon new approaches. To simply coordinate the work may be doable with a managerial mind-set; however, to lead such a team to high performance is a different challenge.

Increased competition is also seen in the governmental services sector including postal, corrections, printing, security, and transit services. Competition from for-profit businesses has heavily encroached upon once-sacred governmental work. In many cases, leadership in the public service sector has responded with transformation. Far from shrinking in the face of challenge, stunning examples of leadership creating superior results exist in many local and national governmental institutions.

Shifting Technology and Social Standards

The rate of change has increased. Where new technology life spans are decreasing, the refinement periods also experience decreases. Incremental improvement on the old technology evaporates as a shift to radical, transformative technology takes place. Think of the audio recording industry, the printing industry, the electronics industry; all attracted new thinkers, people who came into the industry with ideas that revolutionized the technology. And no sooner than a new invention, business innovation, or service novelty comes into existence, the pressure is on to create another. At a minimum, organizational product/service development processes are being transformed with step-function results being experienced in a number of products/services.

These shifts in technology demand transformation. Transforming the way organizations do their daily work as well as the way future planning takes shape is now required. We work with numerous organizations of all types: governmental, large and small for-profits, nongovernmental organizations (NGOs), not-for-profits, social service deliverers, healthcare providers, military, and so on. The strategic planning area, which for some organizations had gained a reputation of b-o-r-i-n-g in previous decades, is now afire within all types of organizations. Given the rapid change of events, market reconfigurations, and short technology cycles, the planning horizons have shifted to near future while more robust, continual planning processes are being established (see Figure 2.1).

The same sweeping shifts are occurring in social systems too. In the battle to attract desirable industry (high community value with a small environmental footprint) into communities, city leaders are rethinking their approaches. *Communities by design* are being formulated to deal with ever increasing complexity and special interest lobbies. Engaged leaders are responding to shifting social agendas by reinventing their people systems. Be it Gen Y, same-sex partners, mobile workforce, spirit in the workplace,

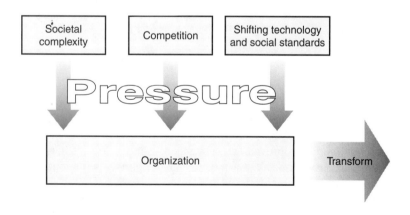

Figure 2.1 Transformative pressure.

or pets-to-work issues, organizations are faced with enormous challenges to move quickly to build and maintain human resources to do the work.

Aircraft manufacturer Boeing Company captured its leadership desires in its *Vision 2016:*

> We will be a world-class leader in every aspect of our business—in developing team leadership skills at every level; in our management performance; in the way we design, build, and support our products; and in our financial results.[4]

Not much new in the words, but Boeing is working to capitalize upon recent transformational approaches to their work. As presented to the authors by John Monroe, director of 777 program management, Boeing radically changed its approach in customer design needs and in its basic customer relationship model.[5] The company also recreated its process of design, manufacturing, and support. By introducing concurrent product and process definition, a modified assembly-line approach, and a host of other new methodologies to aircraft production, Boeing has created, arguably, the best passenger aircraft flying today.

The challenge will be to remain in a transformative leadership stance for the future. The airline industry demands rapid innovation as the economic climate continues to adjust. As a supplier to the airline industry, Boeing will have to reinvent itself again and again if it wishes to fulfill Vision 2016, given competition from Airbus. Airbus's philosophy has a haunting familiarity:

> From the start, Airbus' philosophy has been to listen and respond to customers' needs. New ideas, new techniques and new materials have enabled Airbus to constantly gain market share by building more comfortable, more efficient aircraft that meet passengers' expectations and airlines' business requirements.[6]

The organization that can best produce on its laudable words will have the transformational results as evidence. Like many organizations, these two companies, operating in demanding times, are faced with the reality that past success will only provide a temporary platform from which to initiate radical change. Transformational leadership is now required from nearly all administrations with no skip or leveling out where continuous improvement or standardization takes center stage. Transformation must become a full, permanent partner with continuous improvement and standardization.

Transformation is needed to stay afloat. Breakthrough change and its resulting benefits are required to navigate the shifting waters. Long gone are the days of *same old, same old.* Threats to organizational well-being exist, but transformational opportunities are in abundance. Have a new idea? Jump in and start swimming. There is plenty of space.

VALUE EXCHANGE

Organizations are given a *license to live* at their inception. A number of parties are involved in this birthing process. Some form the organization's charter; others provide resources, give support, or create space in the world for its existence. By choosing to take no action against an organization, political or otherwise, parties grant the organization a license to live. And the organization, formal or informal, arranges agreements with these parties to be born because of the value provided. This arrangement between the organization and the various parties is known as its *value exchange:* the assessment of worth between an organization and all other parties that ensures its continual existence. This worth can be resources, products, ideas, politics, monies, ego enhancement, or compliance (see Figure 2.2).

The individuals, groups, and organizations that grant the license to live receive something in return. If it is a traditional customer/supplier relationship, goods or services are traded for monies. These types of transactions are found in the financial records of the organization. But value exchange is not limited to this simple type of business deal. Some

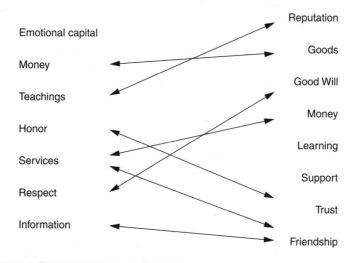

Figure 2.2 Value exchange.

value exchanges consist of support of political ideals by the organization; in turn, no obstruction is exerted to the existence of the organization. For example, animal rights groups formed to remove the license to live of many a furrier in the fur industry. It was not just that members of the animal rights groups stopped buying furs, the simple goods for monies transaction. The animal rights groups yanked the license by influencing others not to buy.

Interestingly enough, value exchange requirements of organizations alter over time. This is because their license to live is negotiated with the outside world—not internally in a closed system. And as discussed earlier, the world is increasing its rate of change and requirements for all organizations to make step-function improvement. As the value exchange is amended, the internal system must adapt or have its license revoked.

Take, for instance, how the postal system's value exchange has been altered. At one time, the exchange was delivery of the mail for a few cents per letter. Then the customer altered the agreement and demanded faster delivery, and then guaranteed timely delivery, secure delivery, and finally tracked delivery. At each stage, the U.S. Postal System had an option to agree or disagree: to honor or not to honor the new value exchange. Consequences in terms of rewards or withdrawal of support were in the balance each time. And if the U.S. Postal System had not responded, its license would have been limited, reduced, or possibly even terminated.

Constantly shifting value exchanges call upon the organizational leadership to be in a continual assessment mode. What are the trends? What are the new requirements and opportunities? And these shifting value exchanges are occurring at an increasing rate due to technological and informational improvements. So following the assessment responses is obligatory. These responses often entail an internal reconstruction of processes, policies, market focus, services or products, and organizational structure. Thus, the need exists for leaders who can transform their organizations due to varying value exchanges.

DELIGHTING IN TRANSFORMATION

Radical change is tough and challenging. You must be conscious of the altering value exchange just to stay alive as an organization. But it is more of a life state than standardization. Changing, adapting, and transforming is more of how people experience life. When looking back, you can see the points of life transformation. You can see how family units have transformed with births, deaths, and changing living environments. Bodies are not standardized, nor in constant continuous improvement mode. They experienced a momentous transformation at conception and through the birthing process and now are heading toward the mysterious transformation of death to post-body existence. The accents of transformation fill people's lives. The choice is whether to embrace the radical changes, building strength and wisdom from each experience, or deny the joy of the ride itself.

It may sound as if transforming has few rewards. But when creativity and the pursuit of life's purpose define the daily mind-set, transformations of many types are seized with vigor in order to move an agenda forward. In this way, transformational leadership is exciting and stimulating—not to be greeted with dread or fear.

SUMMARY LEARNINGS

1. Pressures exist to transform: increased complexity, in technology and social shifts, and increased rate of change negates improvement change alone. Breakthrough change is now required.

2. These pressures have a direct impact on the value the leader and organization has to exchange with the world.

3. The value exchange requirements of all organizations alter over time. This is because their license to live is negotiated with the outside world—not internally in a closed system.

4. As the value exchange is amended, the internal system must adapt or have its license revoked.

TO ACTION

1. What internal or external pressures exist on your organization, creating your call for transformation?

2. Can you compose a value exchange summary for your organization? Who holds your license to live and what are the requirements for continual survival? Think broadly.

3. Can you compose your personal value exchange statement with your organization? What are the exchange elements that allow you to continue in a leadership position, and which parties hold the agreement?

ENDNOTES

1. Elaine L. Wilmore and Cornell Thomas, "The New Century: Is It Too Late for Transformational Leadership?", *Educational Horizons* 79, no. 3 (2002): 115–23.
2. Ibid.
3. David Bohm and Mark Edwards, *Changing Consciousness* (San Francisco: Harper, 1991): 25.
4. www.boeing.com/vision
5. FLEX benchmarking session held at Boeing, Everett, Washington, June 7, 2001.
6. www.airbus.com/about/philosophy.asp

LEADERSHIP VIGNETTE

Greg Delwiche

Leadership Position: Vice president, generation supply

Organization: Bonneville Power Administration (Department of Energy), Portland, Oregon

Transformational Results: Designed, planned, and implemented the transformation of business process systems within the power generation business of Bonneville Power Administration (BPA). BPA launched its Efficiencies Program in order to extract additional power from hydro generation units, better match generation to demand, and improve power tracking and billing. In addition to industrial engineering initiatives, the Efficiencies Program included a revamped information technology system. Greg and his team set out to modernize the entire data stream and ease of information usage for real-time decision making. Efforts paid off with streamlining and optimization of processes, reduced workload, and increased value from the existing asset base at reduced costs. The work continues with significant wins already achieved but with another year of work ahead—and more returns.

Reflections on Transformation[1]

What are your learnings in leading this significant change initiative?

As the leader, I saw the need to transform our business processes and systems in preparation for deregulation by the federal government. I had the opportunity to initiate this change during a good year, and I seized the moment. In hindsight, however, we should have been more comprehensive in broadcasting the value of this initiative to our internal and external stakeholders. They needed to know what we were doing and why—that is our vision and the burning platform for change. In the face of cost-cutting today, this program is viewed by some as a cost, rather than an investment, and we have had to work hard to sway those views. If we had taken the time to build our support during the launch of the program, we would have had more support of the program during these lean years. Also, encouragement is really important. People need to know you value them and that you are proud of them. You can't take the good things for granted.

What were your learnings on personal transformation as part of organizational transformation?

Personally, I am an engineer by training. I am slightly introverted and my natural inclination is that good ideas can sell themselves. However, I have realized the importance of being persistent, to never give up and to keep my eye on the ball. This has led to my success with this project. We've gone from good times to bad, and we have been able to maintain this program by helping people to see that this program is an investment. My leadership approach is to create a strong team, to try and leverage the skills of each person, and to lead in a collaborative way—as opposed to General Patton. As we've gone through radical change, and the recent doubts in these lean years can be very demoralizing to the people involved who have worked so hard to make the change happen, I try to strike a delicate balance in being supportive and encouraging of the team while keeping the steady drum up on progress, pushing the team to deliver 120 percent of the value at 80 percent of the costs.

What about personal transformation of others?

People are at their best in terms of productivity and creativity when they are slightly outside their comfort zone. Most will rise to the challenge and transform themselves to close the gap. This transformation benefits the organization. The transformation of individuals energizes the whole.

How did you reach out beyond BPA and have other people join you in the vision?

We launched a public process to communicate in an interactive way with the entire region. We have held forums with external stakeholders regarding our finances and the projects in which we are engaged. A key lesson, as previously mentioned, is that I should have done more of this earlier, when we launched the program. The support for change you build in the good times will serve you in the bad times too.

Given the current environment, what insights have you gained about the role of creativity?

Creativity is very important in our current environment. Sometimes the closer one is to the nuts and bolts of something, the harder it is to think outside the box. Gaining a fresh perspective is valuable for bringing creativity. We organized our project teams with a project manager responsible for the plan. Our steering committees are comprised of the major clients, and we broadened the committee beyond the direct client organization to enhance the diversity of thinking.

ENDNOTE

1. Transcript excerpts, interview with Greg Delwiche, March 4, 2003, Portland, Oregon, conducted by Tammy Roberts.

3

Transformation toward Organizations of Meaning

Transformational leaders are creating step-function results in an era of rapid shifts of technology and social patterns and increased societal complexity and interdependency. But what does an organization in transformation look like? What kinds of organizations are these leaders guiding their workplaces toward? Are there some models or prototypes that stand out in terms of what types of organizations are being created? In short, yes, there are some common aspects of the organizations experiencing sustainable growth and benchmark results that transformational leaders are targeting. These organizations have a prevailing characteristic of being *organizations of meaning.*

By this phrase, we connote a place where purpose rules, where people and teams operate from a strong sense of intent and common will. A high degree of consciousness prevails in such places, and the power of unleashed spirit is felt all over. The concept of esprit de corps is not restricted to a military unit; it is the standard operating environment in such places. Nor is team spirit a simple idiom or an outdated notion. Are organizations of meaning just never-never land? No, but for many current organizations, the meaning of transformation and step-function change can be envisioned when such a place is compared to the current state.

NATURAL DEVELOPMENT

History helps to understand that organizations of meaning are a natural extrapolation of the performance delivery by organizations and fostered by environmental requirements. At one time, manual labor was the gift of many. A few overseers made sure that labor was applied, and a slow growth of craftsmen as a percentage of the labor force could be found. To greatly simplify history, let's say this occurred during the first 7,000 years of our civilized existence. But as the capacity of the human race to invent and create became steadily greater, complexity emerged, and problems of interdependent systems and inventions became abundant. This takes us through the agricultural era, through the industrial revolution, and into the modern age. In the 1960s and '70s, leadership discovered a vast workforce with untapped brainpower. By and large, the workforce had been trained to be obedient and do as they were told. With the discovery of enormous intellect to better solve problems, management embarked upon transforming the workforce.

At first, using the brainpower and collective intelligence of the entire workforce was optional. Total quality management (TQM) was adopted first by the industrial world, and then by the rest of competitive businesses and governments. TQM brought the intelligence of nonmanagement workers to the table. Initially it was optional, with only the foremost companies and organizations struggling with the concepts in order to achieve a competitive edge. But soon, as the quest for quality was embraced by virtually every organization, the use of a systematic quality approach was no longer optional; it became a requirement for survival. And as companies and governments grew, becoming even more complex and interreliant, the need for something beyond problem solving became apparent. Creativity came on the scene, being in demand for an ever-increasing spectrum of an organization's labor force. Where creativity might have been drawn from top leadership alone, now competitive organizations utilize creativity throughout the supply chain.

The high-tech business sector began to cultivate the creativity of its workforce in the '90s. Going beyond problem solving, the industry asked its people to create, to form new products and services, and to uncover customer wants in areas yet explored. The brisk expansion of the electronics, software, and computing segments was astounding. Creativity extended into the financial systems to raise capital and support operations, even to entice the workforce to remain at an extraordinary level of engagement with their firms. Of course, this story of new market development is still occurring: the boom was extraordinary, the bust disturbing, and the recovery interesting.

Creativity is nearing the point where it will be required of everyone within the workplace. Similar to the engagement of the brain, soon a critical mass of employers will make the creative spirit a requirement. Some would argue that for small or medium for-profit firms, it has already been that way for some time. There is also evidence that larger organizations see the value in encouraging creativity and participation of the workforce as a whole in the reinvention of the company.

As an example, the CEO of IBM, Samuel J. Palmisano, recently shifted key decisions from the long-standing 12-member Corporate Executive Team and invested power deep into teams (strategic, operating, technology) composed of idea people throughout the organization. Additionally, Palmisano took several million dollars from his 2003 bonus and spread it among his top executives in order to emphasize team rewards.[1] Exciting changes undertaken to tap the creative energies of governmental workers are largely underreported. Creativity from the masses is more than a temporal notion designed for selected organization. As its value to produce organizations of meaning is increasingly appreciated, a shift to job requirement is being acknowledged.

ROLE OF SPIRIT

Spirit is a prerequisite for creativity. So similarly to the engagement of labor's minds, the engagement of the spirit is occurring on a broadening basis. Today, leading organizations utilize the creative spirit of their workforce, and more workers are choosing organizations that welcome the whole person—body, brain and spirit (see Figure 3.1).

These organizations may hold a competitive edge today. But soon creating a place where the spirit can thrive will be essential for survival. Both in attracting an enlivened workforce, and in having the organization remain creative and connected in an authentic manner to its customers.

Bringing the whole person to work may be a test, given the fragmented training and development most people have undergone. Work instructions have been to leave private life at home, to separate the concerns of living outside of work to afterwork hours. Some employment programs do address life outside of work, and they are designed to keep the encroachment of the private life from interfering with work life. It is somewhat amazing that the terms *work life* and *private life* even exist. Going back a hundred years or so, this separation would appear nonsensical to the common person. It is hard to imagine a farmer's son expressing to his father that he needed time to work on personal enrichment, develop his physical self, or get in touch with a higher power. Work was integral with life—as sides of life, not separate.

Our highly prized educational system is not based upon the integration of mind, body, and spirit. It remains largely based upon the separation of these three elements into small parts, delivered in subjects or courses. The

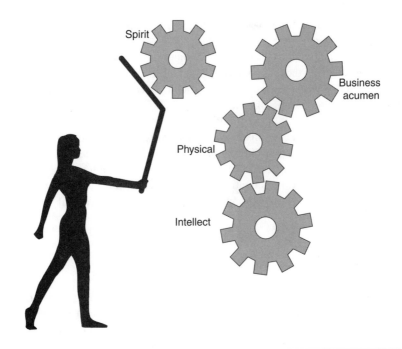

Figure 3.1   Engaging the spirit.

benefit has been focus and depth in comprehending a particular subject. The cost has been influencing individuals to take on the strange outlook of balancing pieces of their lives and failing to connect important subject matters such as ethics and business.

People want to bring the whole person, including the creative spirit, to work. By and large, they want to apply their best to the endeavor. In their book *A Spiritual Audit of Corporate America*, Ian Mitroff and Elizabeth Denton discovered from their research, based upon surveys and more than 90 in-depth interviews with high-level managers and executives, that:

> . . . people do not want to compartmentalize or fragment their lives. The search for meaning, purpose, wholeness, and integration is a constant, never-ending task. It is also a constant, never-ending struggle. To confine this search to one day a week or after hours violates people's basic sense of integrity, of being whole persons. In short, the soul is not something one leaves at home. People want to have their souls acknowledged wherever they go, precisely because their souls accompany them everywhere. They especially

want to be acknowledged as whole persons in the workplace, where they spend the majority of their waking time.[2]

In other words, the basic human instinct is to want to contribute at a much higher level than the typical organization allows. Unfortunately, most people don't have an experience of contributing their best. As noted in Mihaly Csikszentmihalyi's newest book, *Good Business: Leadership, Flow and the Making of Meaning:*

> Most work is either so dull and uninspiring that doing one's best still means using less than 10 percent of one's potentiality, or is so stressful that it sucks that worker's energy dry.[3]

People want to bring their creative juices and invest their spirits. Transformation of the typical organization can provide a favorable environment in producing step-functional results. In organizations of meaning, people bring *their* meaning to the workplace. The workplace does not do the minimum by simply providing the meaning given to the organization by top leadership. A place of purpose is where the meanings of each individual's personal life in the organization align for a collective thrust. Neither manipulation nor temporal coercion, a place of purpose is the expression of the collective spirit.

At the heart of creating an organization of meaning is the leader's view of the individual as a spiritual being. Beyond a human resource or an employee, the organization is a collection of spirits with focus on a particular enterprise. As Wayne Dyer declares, "You are a soul with a body, rather than a body with a soul. You are not a human being having a spiritual experience, but rather a spiritual being having a human experience."[4] When a leader seizes upon this belief with conviction, the workplace will take on a collective meaning. Seeing others as workers employed to perform directed tasks is not only passé, it is terribly limiting.

When spirit is engaged in the daily work, transformation becomes a possibility. Let's see how a problem might yield different responses based upon our engagement of emotion, the mind, and the spirit (see Figure 3.2).

Normally when a problem presents itself, an immediate emotional response emerges in the mind. A proficient manager learns not to overreact or fly off the handle with an emotional response. Although this emotional response may give an instantaneous *feel good* answer for responding to the problem, the probability of a lasting solution is often very low. Analytical abilities are suppressed and a person's foresight is weak, given the emotional charge. For instance, if the person you report to (supervisor, boss, manager, key customer, chairman of the board) came and expressed displeasure with your team's output, based upon what you considered false information, an

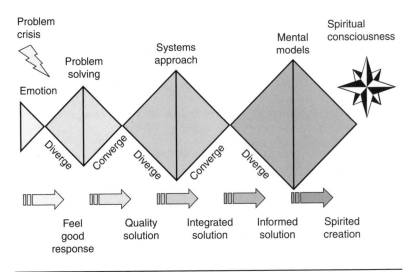

Figure 3.2   Spirited creation model.

immediate emotional response might be to move quickly to the offensive with regard to the source of information. You might say the information came from an unreliable source with questionable motives. Your face may turn red with anger, and you may dismiss the criticism in a raised voice. A *feel good response* has been expressed through your released built-up anger. But this response probably lacks long-term benefits.

By engaging the mind and channeling the emotional response, you could put on your problem-solving hat and begin to seek more lasting quality solutions. Questions begin to flow about the information that formed the basis of the criticism of your team's work. Your problem-solving technique causes a divergence in thinking, away from the convergence of the emotional response. You seek to understand the source of information more as a method of compiling a solution. Longitudinal data is requested. Special causes are noted and control charts are brought forth that demonstrate real improvement, contrary to the charge. A *quality solution* is found in the commitment to share the real results to the hierarchy and to those who initiated the criticism.

But before stopping and giving a solution, you learn that macro systems are at play in daily work. So once again, your mind diverges to consider a systems approach in order to reach an *integrated solution*. What are the communication systems at play? How does information get passed within and outside of the organization? What are the measurement systems, and are they reliable, consistent, and up-to-date? You converge on an integrated solution that has an understanding of organizational complexity and interdependence.

The mind races, expands, and then focuses on possible solutions. And you know the mind's vulnerability based upon the mental models at work. The tendency to lock out information or to embrace new learnings is a matter of mind-set. Shifting responsibility for failure or seeking causal relationships with failure is a mental choice. Understanding mind-sets, you diverge in thinking once again and consider the cultural mind-sets at work in the organization, the mind-sets of the people directly involved, and your own mind-set. Turning the corner and converging on a solution, the result becomes an *informed solution.* You may see that a scarcity mentality of another team may be at the center of the criticism. Unproductive competition for hierarchical approval may have created undeserved condemnation of your team's work. The solution you arrive at is now informed in terms of the mental models at work, integrated with systems thinking, and based upon some variation of the plan–do–study–act improvement approach. Wonderful! And now comes the shift.

Up to this point, we have seen emotion and the mind tackle a problem, an outage in our otherwise peaceful and productive world. The opportunity is to engage conscious spirit. What is it you are at work to create? Where are you going with your chosen vocation, and what is your vision of success? Seeing the problem as an occasion to create, you leave emotion and narrow problem-solving techniques behind. You understand your emotional hot spots and seek system mind-sets that are contributing to the issue. But your focus is on what you wish to create.

The problem at hand simply gives you the chance to create and to bring forth a *spirited creation.* Your spiritual consciousness guides you to seek formation of a vision, not to focus on a barrier or outage. Solving the problem gives way to leveraging the energy at work, even when the energy first appears to be negative in nature. With such a spirit, the number of possibilities seems endless. If the vision is the creation of a more trusting culture in which diverse views can be shared without demeaning others, what an opportunity to roll up your sleeves and dive in. Not with the drive to put out a fire, but to start a fire of trust and openness. This is how daily problems are turned into great creation opportunities. The secret is to have your spirit engaged consciously, knowing why you are in the role as a leader to begin with. The opportunities are unlimited.

Organizations such as Ford Motor Company are better understanding the new fundamentals of organizations of meaning. Chairman William Clay Ford Jr. has delivered a message on the *total leadership* perspective with emphasis on integrating work, home, community, and self.[5] He speaks to having a transformational mind-set, investing in the development of leaders as whole persons. Consistent with the sustainability movement, Ford also captures the growing need to recognize the triple bottom line of financial success, environmental protection, and social responsibility. These are transformational concepts that review the value exchange of the corporation between its license holders and workforce. Eyes are on the results.

SELF, INTERPERSONAL, AND ENTERPRISE MASTERY

The ingredients needed to manifest an organization of meaning may involve structural shifts as shared power, revamped decision making, compensation system overhauls, and reinvention of information methods and channels. Also, a reassessment of archaic motivational practices currently employed may be in line. These practices tend to be more parental than partner in nature. And numerous other considerations need to be taken into account while constructing such powerful places of purpose. But, how to bring into being organizations of meaning is a book by itself. Our inquiry is about the role of leadership in constructing such an organization. And with this disposition, an appreciation of consciousness was first prepared: consciousness of self, relations, and enterprise. Next is the call to move to mastery of each of these perspectives. Each mastery perspective represents a body of knowledge: *self mastery, interpersonal mastery,* and *enterprise mastery* (see Figure 3.3).

Figure 3.3   Mastery perspective ring.

Self Mastery

Knowing how to get the most out of self, the internal self, is a challenge. Whether guided by the Dalai Lama, Gandhi, or Stephen Covey, the task remains with the individual to develop his or her capabilities toward a self-selected purpose. Discovery of a life's purpose is critical and often avoided because the *right* answer does not emerge quickly. In chapter 8, the process of building a *life of meaning* is explored. But at this juncture, it is important to know the role of self mastery in developing a transformational leader.

In his book *The Courage to Teach*, Parker Palmer speaks to knowledge of self over teaching techniques in determining classroom success. He states, "As we learn more of about who we are, we can learn techniques that reveal rather than conceal the personhood from where good teaching comes."[6] Similarly, the transformational leader is most effective when leadership techniques are utilized to enhance the leader within, the drive toward fulfilling a passion. A teacher is most confident and effective when the lesson comes from a state of being. And the leader is most confident and effective when the leadership comes from the spirit expressing itself. The message is to develop inside, to develop personal mastery, which emanates from a strong consciousness of self and life's mission. Then, use method or procedural books to quicken the implementation of the mission—not as the base substance becoming a great transformational leader.

Knowing yourself—your purpose, vision, and values—enables you to lead others. Empowerment requires trust in leadership, a trust that leaders will share their core beliefs openly and honestly. This transparency requires consciousness. Does the leader have knowledge of self? Only with this knowledge can the leader move to the next decision point of disclosing or hiding his or her true self from others.

In the book *What Really Works*, researchers collected 10 years of data about 160 companies covering 200 management practices. Several areas of excellence were found to be determinates of exceptional total return to shareholders. The authors speak to consciousness, truthful representation of beliefs, and the resulting trust:

> When leaders demonstrate their true and firm commitment to their beliefs, they reinforce their leadership roles. Their employees see that the chief executives live by their words, that they can be trusted, and that trust is precious, particularly when times turn hard. No one wants to hear bad news, but it goes down better when it comes from a person you trust.[7]

Self mastery is seen when self-awareness intercepts deep-seated passion. When the drive to live a life of meaning connects with a consciousness of self, the latent potential that resides within each person comes alive. Wisdom is born as experiences are cataloged as learning. Self mastery is not to be confused with mastery of self. Rather it is seizing the mystery of self and life as a whole without fear. If it were a series of a few gates to the road of mastery of self, life would seem boring to the most evolved of our species. Knowing the self is a continual discovery as life and its aging stages blossom.

The Dalai Lama shared his beliefs that awakening a mind is a life's journey and one that is needed when the urgency of death approaches. If people have not developed the skills and wisdom while living, then the panic of the body ending will be painful. But to those who work to develop *right thinking*, the discovery process is transformative. He states:

> The awakening mind is like an elixir that can transform base iron into gold. This is because when we cultivate the awakening mind within ourselves, even our external behavior, the way we speak and the way we behave toward other people can be transformed.[8]

Transformational leaders work to develop an awakened mind. Awakened minds are conscious of a purpose and mature with life's abundant offering. The leader sees transformation as part of the wonderful experiment of life, while others may choose to deaden the mind with chemical abuse, the plug-in drug (television), or meaningless work.

Interpersonal Mastery

Understanding self may be a challenge, but now put this full-time undertaking with knowing others. Interpersonal mastery is not to be confused with mastery of others; it is the mastery of self in relationship to others. As we form relationships to accomplish common objectives, to live in a community, or to simply exist in some state of harmony, the understanding of others is critical. IQ has now been complemented with EQ, with emotional intelligence being granted increasingly higher importance. Each aspect of understanding others calls upon people to examine the self, and the subjects are both broad and deep.

Take, for instance, the subject of trust. As outlined in *The Trust Imperative*, the formation of high-trust relationships mandates the foundation of *trust readiness* within the individual. The concept of trust readiness captures the necessity of knowing and equipping the self as the leverage in building trust with another. The equation states:

> *Trust readiness = trustworthiness* (consistency in action, demonstrated commitment to the endeavor, and forthrightness of capabilities) + *trust willingness* (willingness to invest the energy, willingness to examine assumptions, and willingness to risk).[9]

There is a lot of work captured in this equation, and all this work is for one aspect of relationship building. Consider the other facets of relations such as communications, support, caring, compassion, and love. Each inter-related feature of a relationship will involve considerable insights of self with others. It is enough to cause both IQ and EQ functions to lock up the human brain's hard drive.

When understanding self in relationship to others reaches a sufficient level of performance, then the leap to seeing the relationship as an identity in and of itself is possible. The relationship has a voice, one beyond the two combined individual voices. This is where one and one can add up to one. The two distinct voices remain—and a single new entity emerges that has its own characteristics and identity. This is from where newly formed power emanates. Transformational leaders know how to tap into this power. They know the voice of the relationship and develop and plan to its contribution.

Enterprise Mastery

Knowing the value exchange of the endeavor and obtaining the acumen of the industry or field are part of enterprise mastery. The transforma-tional leader must bring about an awareness of the undertaking to the extended system. And to accomplish this task, the leader must not only know the trade of today, but also how environmental forces are shaping it for the future.

If the trade is humanitarian aid, a mastery level entails knowing how to best deliver and sustain the target of the aid. What are the most efficient, effective methods of helping others? How does such an operation obtain necessary support and supplies from governmental, private, and public institutions? What are the trends in the field? What are the best-in-class nongovernmental organizations and out-of-industry benchmarks? What is the language of humanitarian aid, and in what direction is the leader shap-ing the language? For these types of questions, a transformational leader would have ready answers filled with tremendous knowledge, but at the same time, being a receptor of new information and approaches. Thus is the description of a master. Not one that has learned it all, but one that seeks the integration of subject matter and searches for increased knowledge and better approaches.

Given financial expertise and appointment within a for-profit busi-ness, enterprise mastery would encompass fiscal acumen. However, this would be but a start. The transformational leader would have mastery knowledge and appreciation of the entire enterprise, going beyond a par-ticular role. What is the value exchange of the enterprise? How is this value exchange tending to modify in the near future? What are the intangibles that keep customers engaged? What aspects of relationship management are most applicable to the extended system culture? Questions like these occupy the mind of the transformational leader looking to make the step-functional leap in results. Acquired learnings from an MBA, financial degree, or other qualifications can help, but are a poor substitute for the required knowledge. It is not unusual to find persons who can talk the language but fail in the deeper comprehension of the trade, bordering on incompetence. The phrase *articulated incompetence* speaks to the ability to talk the jargon without any results. Unfortunately, articulated incompetence is a common finding.

Along with self mastery and interpersonal mastery, enterprise mastery offers a lifetime of discovery. Businesses, governmental services, and NGOs live in a tumultuous sea of change. Excitement, exuberance, and fulfillment are descriptors used by transformational leaders engaged in this revolutionary environment. Far from expressions of anxiety, fear, and personal concern uttered by some, the transformational leader seeks turbulent and chaotic circumstances as opportunities to accelerate operational results. Where there is disruption, there lies a prospect for discontinuous improvement.

SUMMARY LEARNINGS

1. Organizations of meaning are created by having leaders of purpose building an organization comprised of people of purpose.

2. Purpose emanates from spirit, which is sought after for its energy and sustainability value.

3. Organizations of meaning have been found to be beneficial environments for repeated transformational change. Rapid and fundamental changes in an organization's macro systems are embraced by a transformative organization in order to fulfill its purpose.

4. Self mastery, interpersonal mastery, and enterprise mastery form the perspective ring. Each requires considerable skill and effort to develop, and the process is never-ending.

TO ACTION

1. What is your life's purpose? What is your reason for being? Capture your response in writing.

2. How does your leadership focus and the work you do fulfill your life's purpose? Capture your response in writing.

3. How well do you know your self? On a scale of 1–10 assess your self across the three perspectives: self mastery, interpersonal mastery, and enterprise mastery. What are your strengths? Where are your learning opportunities?

4. Is there a separation of work life and personal life at your workplace? While engaged in dialog with people at your workplace, listen for the degree to which separation of work life and personal life takes place.

ENDNOTES

1. Spencer E. Ante, "The New Blue," *Business Week* (March 17, 2003): 80–88.
2. Ian I. Mitroff and Elizabeth A. Denton, *A Spiritual Audit of Corporate America* (San Francisco: Jossey-Bass, 1999): xv.
3. Mihaly Csikszentmihalyi, *Good Business: Leadership, Flow and the Making of Meaning* (New York: Viking Penguin, 2003): 30.
4. Wayne W. Dyer, *You'll See It When You Believe It: The Way to Personal Transformation* (New York: Harper Collins, 2001): 2.
5. Stewart D. Friedman, "Leadership DNA: The Ford Motor Story," *Training and Development* 55, no. 3 (2001): 22–29.
6. Parker J. Palmer, *The Courage to Teach* (San Francisco: Jossey-Bass, 1998): 24.
7. William F. Joyce, Nitin Nohria, and Bruce Roberson, *What Really Works: The 4 + 2 Formula for Sustained Business Success* (New York: HarperCollins, 2003): 201.
8. Dalai Lama, *The Joy of Living and Dying in Peace* (San Francisco: HarperCollins, 1997): 21.
9. Stephen K. Hacker and Marsha Willard, *The Trust Imperative* (Milwaukee: ASQ Quality Press, 2001): 34.

4

Leadership's Uniqueness

Transformational leadership transcends "either/or" thinking and requires the leader to embody both leadership and management talent. Hence, in the next few chapters, we will explore the differences between management and leadership, drawing them together to articulate the uniqueness of transformation leadership.

Leadership differs from management, but because the overlap and the complementary relationship are so strong, the distinctions are often misplaced in the heat of organizational change. The result of forgetting leadership's uniqueness creates confusion within the organization and poor placement of talents. R.W. Griffin states the differences in this manner:

> Organizations need both management and leadership if they are to be effective. Leadership is necessary to create change, and management is necessary to achieve orderly results. Management in conjunction with leadership can produce orderly change, and leadership in conjunction with management can keep the organization properly aligned with its environment.[1]

Different skill sets, but they are complementary. Management is more of the mind, overseeing operations and using energies to ensure delivery of expected value. Leadership, on the other hand, is more of the spirit, a creative expression through others. Both are critical to the long-term success of any organization.

MANAGING SYSTEMS

Management is continually needed to keep organizational systems in place and to apply the energy necessary to overcome entropy. Without management, systems would atrophy and cease to produce intended outcomes.

In the not so distant past, the term *manager* was exclusively applied to one who oversaw people. As it turned out, some managers were leaders and some were not. It was observed that the people being managed were engaged in a process to produce something, and therefore, the manager worked with others to maintain or improve the system. While it was desired that the manager be concerned with the system and subsystems, leadership was the service increasingly demanded from the person in such a role. And labor was increasingly asked to manage their work. High performance work systems (HPWS) helped with this redefinition as workers with the capabilities to manage systems and subsystems were identified, giving the once-manager time to lead. So management was opened to a whole host of people, whether they had a title or not. People who saw the inputs, outputs, and internal converting processes of system management were given new responsibilities—to manage their systems. Thus, we define *management* as *the stewardship of organizational systems including their maintenance, standardization, and improvement.*

As part of their focus, managers provide analysis and documentation of their systems. By involving customers and suppliers, a manager better meets quality requirements. Managers are required to standardize their systems and to remove unwanted variation. Standardization is a valuable task, and when coupled with system improvement, it forms a granite operational foundation.

Many leaders underestimate the amount of work and dedication required just to keep an organization going. Appreciation of this work would serve leaders well. Often, as these leaders speak to change, the managers holding up the current organization feel disenfranchised.

The primary domain of the manager can be found inside the organization, attending to systems and working to establish robustness within. This does not mean the manager is insensitive to the outside. Clearly, systems have external customers and suppliers as well as internal ones. But the average manager spends a majority of his or her time on efforts focused internally to keep the systems running and the organization functioning. Likewise, improvement is warranted, but standardization is the first order (see Figure 4.1).

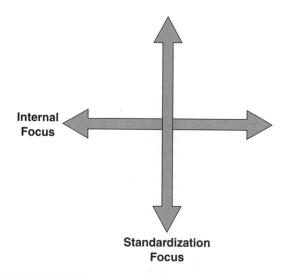

Internal
Focus

Standardization
Focus

Figure 4.1 Internal and standardization domain.

LEADING ORGANIZATIONS

Where management works primarily on systems and subsystems, ensuring their performance per design, leaders are asked to focus on taking the organization forward. Vision and creativity are leveraged through empowering others and building community. Their primary focus is charting the way onward for the organization within the context of external forces and opportunities. Seeing the needed changes to generate a healthy value exchange with the external environment, the domain of change is the foremost concern of the leader. Where to lead, how to reconstruct the organization, and who to productively involve are all part of the leader's interest. Therefore, the principle domains of the leader are external, and focused on change.

While the leader's concentration is on the external and change, a certain degree of expertise must be exhibited internally and toward system integrity. The ability to appreciate both ends of the continuum, the tension between standardization and change, is easier said than done as it requires the transformational leader to embrace two divergent mind-sets, one that

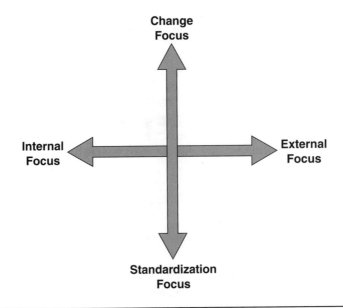

Figure 4.2   Transformational leader's domain.

flourishes in chaos and the other that fosters order (see Figure 4.2). These two mind-sets are most often found in different individuals, rather than together in one person. This idea is supported by Abraham Zaleznik in his article, "Managers and Leaders: Are They Different?" Zaleznik states:

> The crucial difference between managers and leaders lies in the conception they hold, deep in their psyches, of chaos and order. Leaders tolerate chaos and lack of structure and are thus prepared to keep answers in suspense, avoiding premature closure on important issues. Managers seek order and control and are almost compulsively addicted to disposing of problems even before they understand their potential significance.[2]

Now, this is not a sleight of hand. For the leader to be effective, a healthy management competency must be demonstrated. Not to take over the duties of others, not even to perform to the same managerial performance level, but the requirement is to be proficient in management science. Otherwise, the functional expertise being led is an unknown. So the transformational leader must have an eye on the internal and standardization domain.

TAKING A LEAD: LESSONS FROM THE ANIMAL KINGDOM

The uniqueness of the leader's role, especially the transformational leader, can sometimes get lost in models and descriptors. We have found in our workshops and public addresses that metaphors are at times helpful. Comparing three common styles of individual and collective leaderships with some prey and predators of the animal kingdom might offer a fresh perspective.

The zebra offers insight into the least effective leadership style—one that is still visible in many organizations. Do you know why zebras have stripes? We did not until asking a guide on an African safari. A zebra's stripes allow for an interesting defense. When zebras are being chased, they stay within a herd formation allowing their patterned bodies to overlap. This confuses the predator. The key to a predator's attack strategy is to single out one particular victim among the entire herd. But with the visual impact of overlapping striped patterns, the predator finds this difficult. The predator is confused, not knowing where one zebra starts and another ends.

Blending in to not become a target is used too often by top teams and middle management as a leadership style. Making sure the individual is not picked off becomes the primary goal. Operating out of defensiveness can produce some level of results, but this style is insufficient to lead transformational change.

Certainly a cheetah takes a leadership position in its pursuit of prey. As a lone hunter, the cheetah is often victorious in accomplishing the end result; however, the percentage of kills versus attacks is low. Speed is the cheetah's advantage. Built for speed, it can accelerate from zero to 40 mph in three strides and to its full speed of 70 mph in seconds. As the cheetah runs, only one foot at a time touches the ground. And with its 20- to 25-foot stride, there are times when no feet touch the ground. It waits, watches, and stalks. Finally it strikes with amazing speed, tripping up the back legs of its prey and killing by using its powerful jaw with a clamping action on the prey's throat. Alone in its quest, it is self-reliant while at the same time being limited in what it can accomplish.

African wild dogs hold insights into how a top team could better lead. These animals work as a team to bring down prey many times their size. By tracking the prey and refusing to stop their pursuit, they run the prey to a point of exhaustion and then collectively bring it down. In their collective perseverance and tenacity, they achieve the goal. In comparison to an attack by a cheetah, which succeeds about three out of ten attempts, the wild dogs' approach brings home dinner about seven out of ten times.

African wild dogs have another important trait allowing them to be successful hunters, creativity. African wild dogs adapt to new environments in ways that create opportunity. With electric fences surrounding animal reserves, it is not unusual to see the dogs herd enormous antelope into the fence, causing the prey to be temporarily stunned. In this manner, the dogs, acting quickly, can take down a beast they otherwise would have been unable to kill. (See sidebar for more details.)

RECOGNIZING EFFECTIVE LEADERS

Leaders are not zebras. They do not look to blend in for protection. Eating grass on the plain, taking care of the business for today in a passive, heads-down manner may have its benefits, but it is not leadership. And when change presses in, the desire to run away or to avoid conflict points to a longing to return to the status quo.

Cheetahs are great for getting a herd to move. The lightning-fast strike provides for drama and excitement. It is truly magnificent to see; like a flash of energy, cheetahs really know how to get the herds jumping. Leadership, yes! If only an organization could respond and change overnight while the electricity is still in the air. But organizations, like the herd, have a predictable way of beating this style of leadership many more times than not. The herd will simply move away with a few individuals having a close call. And as the cheetah tires, the organization returns to near normal conditions, grazing on the plains.

Transformational leadership combines hunter instincts with teamwork and tenacity. Like the wild dogs of Africa, transformational leaders have the stamina to pursue breakthrough change. They persist in their commitment to move ahead while the sun is shining and even when the nights are dark and lonely.

Identifying and differentiating between a zebra, cheetah, and wild dog is rather easy. But do the characteristics of a wild dog really demonstrate superior performance? Well, some research time was spent on this question. The research project conducted by John Chuka and Dr. Marvin Washington investigated the African Wild Dog Theory as postulated by Marvin Washington and Stephen Hacker in their article "New Directions in Team Effectiveness: Lessons from the Wild Dogs of Africa." They hypothesized that *shared leadership, shared vision, tenacity,* and *individual skills* enhance the effectiveness of work groups, with respect to their performance. They mentioned high performance traits as identified in African wild dogs to explain why the African wild dogs, as predators, achieve more success than lions and cheetahs with respect to hunting down their prey and keeping it for food.

WILD DOGS

We are constantly on the lookout for wild dogs. The characteristics that emerge from newsworthy individuals, biographies, and within organizations demonstrate outstanding results. But it is amazing where you can find wild dogs when you are simply on alert. On a recent excursion into Tuli Block, located along the Limpopo River, in Botswana, we came across just such a tenacious spirit. Imagine a high desert with scattered shrubs, sparse small trees, and savanna grasses. Beautiful country but scarcely populated, Botswana has one of the world's lowest population densities.

The accidental discovery of a wild dog began with an automobile accident. Traveling upon a secondary road to a lodge, we had hoped to make better time. After four hours we weren't quite sure of our location, but the dirt road was the only way forward. Suddenly, we saw a rock in the middle of the road, and our responsive decision was to drive dead-center over the rock to avoid damaging the front end. Unfortunately, the vehicle was a few centimeters too low, and it bottomed out, creating a tremendous oil leak. In less than a mile, the engine had been drained of its precious lubricant. Our minds rushed from an adventurous spirit to considerable worry. We knew that the nearest village with any sort of repair station was 50 miles in any direction. In fact, the last village we had encountered an hour ago consisted of a lone food shop with some gas pumps.

Luckily, we had just admired a rare grouping of buildings about three miles back. We left the automobile and hiked to what we discovered to be an ostrich ranch. Hundreds of birds were visible in large pens. Construction material, consisting of fencing material, concrete bricks, and irrigation piping, was strewn around. Mike Hallam was the owner. He and his family had been ordered to vacate their Zimbabwean ranch in the central district less than a year previously. The politically orchestrated destruction of an idyllic community had come crashing down, causing him to start again, virtually from scratch, in Tuli Block.

As we approached the ranch house, his wife Moira met us on the small lawn of their home. We must have been a sight coming from nowhere, with nothing but the clothes on our back. We were refugees in a sense, with no place to stay, and helpless. We were welcomed as

Continued

Continued

guests, and during the period it took to arrange a tow and transport from the capital city of Gaborone 200 miles away, we learned to admire what Mike and Moira had created.

In a few months, they had transported their birds to a foreign country, losing less than 25 percent on the journey. They built living quarters for themselves and three additional families from the ruins of a dilapidated farm and provided housing for 11 Zimbabwean ranch hands that accompanied them out of the chaos and for a dozen or so Botswana that joined in creating a phoenix. A new building was being constructed, for the egg incubators he had successfully transported out of Zimbabwe. New bore holes and a river pump were in different stages of completion as the new community worked intensively to provide water for irrigating a feed crop and to provide for the birds.

The bureaucratic hurdles to secure loans, land lease, operating licenses, and the purchasing and delivery of construction materials served as sources of frustration. But like wild dogs, Mike had persevered. He pushed the system for obtaining the critical items needed to launch the ranch. And looking down the time line, he envisioned beyond the breeding and production of ostrich meat to the production of feed grain, cattle, vegetables, and crocodile breeding. These were all opportunities that the land and market forces presented to him. Mike was an opportunist moving forward with a strategic design, going after the readily available prey to meet a specific need.

A transformational leader also cultivates other leaders, thus developing a whole pack of wild dogs. So within the first few months of his arrival, Mike brought in another rancher to lead his up and coming cattle business. Another exiled Zimbabwean friend served as a general foreman. Moria temporarily worked as an accountant at a chicken farm some miles away to bring in much needed cash, and then on her off hours, she maintained the books for their ranch. They were all leaders in their own right, on the hunt and taking the point when required.

Community-building is one of the most visible leadership skills. You see the outputs so easily. Mike Hallam had reproduced a vibrant community, which had been part of his past. He chose not to focus on the past injustice, but rather looked forward, creating a meaningful life. Although discovered by accident, we departed from our hosts' ranch invigorated by our encounter with a wild dog.

The sample population for this research study was 336 undergraduate business seniors who enrolled in one of two strategic management classes at a major university in the Southwest. Besides the lectures, the students, in groups of two to five, were required to participate in an airline business simulation exercise. Their performance in this exercise is directly reflected in profit they make as a group at the end of the exercise: a group is considered successful if it made a profit of $800,000 or more. A questionnaire was designed and administered to the sample population to investigate the degree that groups exhibiting wild dog traits (shared vision, leadership, tenacity, individual skills) were more likely to be successful than groups that did not exhibit these traits.

The findings generated by computer-based analyses, using the statistical software called *STATA*, suggest that three of the four traits were significant predictors of team success:

1. Teams that have shared vision will be more effective than teams that do not have shared vision.

2. Teams that have tenacity will be more effective than teams that do not have tenacity.

3. Teams that have individual skills will be more effective than teams that do not have individual skills.

One other interesting fact was observed. In addition to these three traits, teams that thought they were going to be successful were indeed successful. With respect to our wild dog traits, they found that teams with high levels of shared leadership were more likely to report that they thought their team would be successful, which predicted success. Thus, in support for all wild dog traits, only shared leadership is mediated by a belief in success.

Identifying superior leaders versus average leaders who may be great managers has proven more difficult. In the next chapter, we take a further step in understanding the characteristics and skills of great managers.

DIFFERING LEADERSHIP FRAMEWORKS

Many different types of leadership frameworks exist in the quest to discover the secrets of leadership effectiveness, and the realization that differing situations call for particular skills (situational leadership) was a breakthrough in leadership science. The concept of polarity management moved the body of knowledge even further. Barry Johnson describes this notion as:

Polarities to manage are sets of opposites which can't function well independently. Because the two sides of a polarity are interdependent, you cannot choose one as a "solution" and neglect the other. The objective of *polarity management* is to get the best of both opposites while avoiding the limits of each.[3]

Polarity management, or what we would prefer to call *polarity leadership,* allows for an either/or mind-set to become a both/and mind-set. For instance, flexible and rigid competing leadership character poles could be seen as *either/or.* But when clarity of vision and direction is needed, along with the flexibility to alter the course based on shifting environmental concerns, the desire is to have a leader that is both flexible and rigid, a *both/and* position.

The competing values framework[4] integrates contradictory leadership roles into one single framework, emphasizing the need for the leader to have some level of mastery in all opposing roles in order to successfully fulfill competing expectations.

The research of Olivia Yang and Eric Shao hypothesizes a positive relationship between team effectiveness and the balance of eight supervisory roles. A competing values leadership instrument was used to measure the eight supervisory roles within self-managed teams. When the competing values approach was placed within an environment of shared leadership, the finding reinforced the need for opposing roles in self-managed teams. Yang and Shao explain:

> The results show that effective self-managed teams play and balance the eight competing roles. Moreover, a team's lifecycle has an impact on the priority of the competing roles. The findings indicate that managers in the organizations should not only be concerned about the development and balance of the eight roles, but should also change role emphasis during the different stages in the team development.[5]

These frameworks are but a few from which we drew key principles in building the forthcoming transformational leadership model.

SUMMARY LEARNINGS

1. Management is different from leadership in that management is about controlling and predicting, while leadership is about creation. Both are important.

2. Hiding out as a manager puts the organization at risk.

TO ACTION

1. Can you identify times when you have hidden in the crowd, embarked on change as a loner, or joined a team of change agents? What were the results?

2. Can you identify the zebras, cheetahs, and wild dogs in your organization?

3. What is your capacity to hold a both/and mind-set? What prevents you from considering divergent points of view?

ENDNOTES

1. Rick W. Griffin, *Fundamentals of Management: Core Concepts and Applications* (Boston: Houghton Mifflin, 2003): 304.
2. Abraham Zaleznik, "Managers and Leaders: Are They Different?" *Harvard Business Review, A Collection of Articles: Best of HBR on Leadership: Balancing Stability and Change* (Boston, MA: Harvard Business School Publishing, Product Number 8288, 2001): 11.
3. Barry Johnson, *Polarity Management: Identifying and Managing Unsolvable Problems* (Amherst, MA: HRD Press, 1992): xii.
4. Robert Quinn et al., *Becoming a Master Manager: A Competency Framework* (New York: John Wiley & Sons, 1996): 13.
5. Olivia Yang and Y. Eric Shao, "Shared Leadership in Self-Managed Teams: A Competing Values Approach," *Total Quality Management* 7, Issue 5 (1996): 14, 521.

LEADERSHIP VIGNETTE

Doug Beigel

Leadership Position: Chief executive officer

Organization: COLA, Columbia, Maryland

Organizational Focus: Healthcare sector, not-for-profit organization performing medical laboratory quality audits and accreditations.

Transformational Results: Formed in 1978, and after growing to command percentage of the market, increased market pressure and declining revenue drove the organization into living off reserves with an insolvency slope of less than four years. Doug drove home the urgency of COLA's condition to employees and board, established energizing vision, built new alliances in new market segments including international expansion, and abruptly turned losses into positive cash flow. Created a tremendous sense of abundant opportunities with speedy bottom line impact versus the shrinking market, *enemy at the gate* previous culture.

Reflections on Transformation[1]

What are the learnings you have on creating a burning platform for change?

It was critical to focus each individual and team on the fact that if we did not change, really bad things would happen—the organization would cease to exist. Staying where we were was not an option. A visual representation of the burning platform for change made a big impression on all—including the board. The picture helped people not question the fact of the looming crisis, but rather drove them to look forward.

What where your learnings on personal transformation as part of organizational transformation?

It started with me—with my understanding of *my* connection to the burning platform results and the trouble we faced. I personally did not want to live in the current picture. What I valued was not represented in the current picture. I looked at my options, got clear with my purpose and what excited me, dropped the cautions of the past, and moved forward.

What about personal transformation of others?

Not an easy process for others when they are working with a leader who wants to move aggressively forward. First, I found the need to bring the values to mind and keep them alive in the transition. Secondly, I observed that it took time for many to move forward, off the burning platform, until I made clear the BHAG (big, hairy, audacious goal). Once the BHAG was given and internalized, people moved forward and individual transformations began. Some found that their interests did not align with our new direction. My experience was that, for some, the discovery of the misalignment led to a declaration of the nonfit and then resignation. These separations were not unpleasant in a strange way. Both parties, COLA and the individuals, saw the separation as basically the right thing to do and, in fact, several business alliances have formed post-separation. Others were asked to leave, departing in denial and confusion.

How did you reach out beyond COLA and have other people join you in the vision?

Sharing vision was most important, being excited about the opportunities. This is not to say we ignored the barriers. But I offered others the opportunity to go to the mountain with me, to share in our vision of improving healthcare worldwide. I offered other organizations in the business, yes, even some seeming adversaries the chance to join the drive to the vision. We built a new community. For the most part, I found that if others were attracted to the vision and had similar values, strong and enduring relationships followed. But when the values were not in alignment, the relationships were not formed. For instance, when the motivation to improve healthcare was discussed and greed was declared, the lack of common values was evident.

ENDNOTE

1. Transcript excerpts, interview with Doug Beigel, January 24, 2003, Columbia, Maryland, conducted by Stephen Hacker and Tammy Roberts.

5

What Makes a Great Manager?

In the previous chapter, we defined management as the *stewardship of organizational systems, including their maintenance, standardization, and improvement.* Within his or her stewardship role, the great manager sets goals for his or her business unit, establishes a predictable path to achieving those goals, improves upon or controls work processes, and solves problems when deviation from desired results occurs.

Within this context of overseeing existing operations and ensuring predictability of results, the manager's view of leadership is limited to the current reality. Rather than charting new territory into the unknown, inspired by vision, passion, creativity, and risk-taking, great managers excel at getting others to work together toward achieving a predictable, defined goal. Abraham Zaleznik in his article "Managers and Leaders: Are They Different?" captures the role of manager within organizations:

> A managerial culture emphasizes rationality and control. Whether his or her energies are directed toward goals, resources, organization structures, or people, a manager is a problem solver. The manager asks: What problems have to be solved, and what are the best ways to achieve results so that people will continue to contribute to this organization? From this perspective, leadership is simply a practical effort to direct affairs; and to fulfill his or her task. A manager requires that many people operate efficiently and effectively at different levels of status and responsibility. It takes neither genius nor heroism to be a manager, but rather persistence, tough-mindedness, hard work, intelligence, analytical ability, and perhaps most important, tolerance and goodwill.[1]

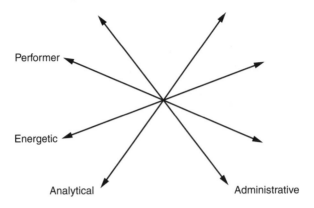

Figure 5.1   Manager's domain for characteristics.

Great managers are clear about their personal fit within the overall organization and the fit of their system or subsystem within the larger context of the organization's mission, vision, and strategic directions. They understand their value to the organization and capitalize on their credibility and reputation as a star performer. Possessing expert knowledge of a business system or systems, they use this knowledge to influence the organizational infrastructure and planning and budgeting processes to best position themselves to achieve results for which they are directly accountable.

Great managers have a number of unique talents and skills fundamental to their achievement. These talents are embodied in four characteristics of great managers: administrative, analytical, performer, and energetic. We have taken the opportunity to rethink and redefine these traditional, often-used terms looking through the lens of a *conscious* manager, a manager who is self-aware, alive with personal purpose, and has clear personal vision, knowledge, and commitment to the organization's mission (see Figure 5.1).

SELF, INTERPERSONAL, AND ENTERPRISE MASTERY

Before addressing each of the fundamental characteristics of great managers, let us describe their relationship to the three mastery perspectives. As noted in chapter 3, each mastery perspective represents a body of knowledge: self mastery, interpersonal mastery, and enterprise mastery. One can view each of the four managerial characteristics from the point of view of self, relationship to others, and the endeavor of the enterprise.

For example, at the level of the individual, one could ask these questions: What are my strengths and weaknesses in terms of administration of my own life? What areas of my life am I driving for predictable results? What is the quality of my planning or budgeting? Does my planning produce desired results? Where am I not taking corrective action when variation exists between my plan and current results?

Similarly, in relationship to others, these questions can be answered: Are we conscious of a common, well-defined goal, and are we administering our relationship to achieve that goal? In the case of marriage, what are our goals? Is the relationship conscious of the role of planning and budgeting to achieve desired goals? How is our life organized to achieve predictability, and are we organized in a way that makes rational sense? On the job, similar questions could be asked by a chartered team. In fact, team charters often reflect how the team will organize or administer itself to achieve the desired output.

At the level of enterprise, ask these questions: Are you conscious of how your system or subsystems fit with the enterprise's reason for being? Do you organize and manage your system or subsystem to achieve the vision, mission, and strategic direction set by the top leadership, or are you managing your own personal dynasty? As top leaders of the organization, do your managers manage the organization toward its endeavor, and do they have the managerial skills needed to be successful? How are you enhancing managerial talent within your organization? Are you promoting the right people with the right talents to the right job?

Generally, the following characteristics are addressed from the perspective of enterprise mastery. As you consider each one, reflect on how each characteristic would be viewed through the lens of self and interpersonal mastery.

ADMINISTRATIVE

Great managers are acknowledged experts on the internal workings of the organization. Said simply, they know how to get work done and are highly skilled in moving their agenda forward. They use existing processes in the drive for predictable results that are consistent with the organization's established goals. Their primary role in the organization is to reduce variation and incrementally improve current business processes using standardization and continuous process improvement tools.

Great managers are experts in planning and budgeting. Planning and budgeting by great managers occurs within the boundaries of the strategic directions and vision set by top leaders of the organization. Frequently, organizations confuse the terms planning and budgeting with setting the organizational vision and direction. These activities are different in participation, goals, and approach. As noted by John Kotter in his article "What Leaders Really Do":

> Setting direction is never the same as planning or even long-term planning. Planning is a management process, deductive in nature and designed to produce orderly results, not change. Setting direction is more inductive. Leaders gather a broad range of data and look for patterns, relationships, and linkages to help explain things. What's more the direction-setting aspect of leadership does not produce plans, it creates vision and strategies.[2]

The best managers possess the capacity to see the inner workings and needs of the entire organization, but when it comes to planning and budgeting, they often focus on the needs of their own system or subsystem. This has resulted in the frequent use of the term *silo thinking* by top leaders frustrated and critical of the narrowly-formed mind-set of many managers.

Great managers constantly seek information about their organization and how it works. As brokers of information, they use their formal and informal networks to positively influence others toward the advancement of their agenda, as you will see later in this chapter. They are highly skilled at project management, creating step-by-step plans for achieving goals.

Great managers are responsible for organizing and staffing, setting up the infrastructure for accomplishing the organization's objectives. According to J. Kotter:

> Managers organize to create human systems that can implement plans as precisely and efficiently as possible. These decisions are much more like architectural decisions. It's a question of fit within a particular context.[3]

The focus on the infrastructure is to efficiently and effectively organize people so that goals can be met with minimal risk and predictable results. J. Kotter further states that:

> Managerial processes must be as close as possible to fail-safe and risk-free. That means they cannot be dependent on the unusual or hard to obtain. The whole purpose of systems and structures is to help normal people who behave in normal ways to complete routine jobs successfully, day after day.[4]

Unlike leaders, managers are risk-averse. In fact, in most cases, their job doesn't require them to undertake risks or to venture into the unknown.

Instead, they keep a close watch on what's known. They ensure that a system functions as it should: producing desired, predictable outputs.

ENERGETIC

Many great managers have a large capacity to find and employ energy from within and to use this energy to knock down barriers to getting the job done. The perpetual energy of the *conscious* manager is actually an expression of their unique spirit and a strong connection of their vocation to that life purpose. This is not to say that the *unconscious* manager is absent of energy. In fact, many managers have a good deal of energy, but often that energy can wane during the most turbulent times. In the unconscious manager, energy is often derived from ego that, when no longer fed, diminishes.

The depth of the spring of energy available to a great manager is at its deepest when connected to the person's understanding of a larger purpose for self and their connection to the larger world. Clarity of personal purpose, personal vision, and values are critical to accessing, sustaining, and renewing energy from within. The strength of the bond between individual purpose and the organization's endeavor serves as a powerful flywheel of energy.

One's individual relationship to the world also plays a powerful role in one's ability to source energy from within. Some people do not see themselves connected to the world, particularly with their role in creating the pain, frustrations, and problems they have in life. These individuals live at the mercy of the events of life. They live in hope that good fortune will eventually come their way. *At-effect* individuals see themselves as victims. They believe things happen to them. They experience events as occurring outside of their control. This view of the world is an emotional and mental drain on one's life energy.[5]

Other people choose to see their connection to all that surrounds them. Their primary mental model is one of creation. They see themselves as accountable for making things happen around them: the good, the bad, and the ugly. These individuals own it all, both the failures and the achievements. This *at-cause* view of the world can powerfully sustain the source of a person's life energy. Rather than experiencing depletion of energy as a result of failure and problems, at-cause individuals use each opportunity to learn and to grow stronger. This is possible because their view of the world is that they themselves created the disappointment or failure. Great managers take failure in stride and are renewed with energy through learning discovery.

ANALYTICAL

Great managers have keen analytical ability. They are rational, logical human beings seeking to create order. They see patterns and cause-and-effect relationships, which allow them to predict reasons for performance, and conversely, for failed performance.

Performance management systems can be particularly powerful in bringing focus to several meaningful indicators that allow managers to understand how well the organization is performing. Great managers monitor results against the plan to ensure that progress is being made.

Using their analytical skills, the best managers demonstrate great problem-solving ability. Different from creativity, problem solving includes trying to make something go away. The mind-set is one of fixing or doing away with. They are focused on how to get things done efficiently and effectively, and this also applies to problem solving. This often results in solutions that are more process, or tactical, in nature. Rarely do managers transcend the problem itself to seek a higher-order solution.

PERFORMER

Great managers have the ability to establish personal and unit goals within the context of the organization's endeavor. Bringing their rational, logical mind to any situation, they can set the agenda and the logical plan to move from *A* to *Z*, including measures for success. They are highly confident in their ability to perform as they have a demonstrated track record.

In addition to the ability to develop masterful performance management systems, the great manager can predict whether his or her system or subsystem will meet targets. Generally, targets for performance are established based on past performance, with incremental improvement being assumed by the manager.

Managers build networks throughout the organization to assist them in advancing their own agenda and to achieve specific goals. Conscious managers set their agenda consistent with the goals of the organization. It is important to note that great managers build networks for the purpose of meeting their own specific objectives. It's about getting *their* job accomplished. They are sophisticated influencers, brokers, and horse traders in gaining the support of others within the organization to move their agenda forward. Kotter explains:

> Effective general managers allocate significant time and effort toward developing a network of cooperative relationships among people they feel are needed to satisfy their emerging agendas.[6]

Leaders, on the other hand, build community by looking both internally and externally for people of shared purpose and vision. They build relationships based on common values and principles, seeking alignment for collective action.

THE IMPORTANCE OF MANAGERIAL SKILLS IN LEADERSHIP

The four managerial traits are fundamental to leading an organization of meaning. What is required of the transformational leader is not a management *or* leadership construct but rather a management *and* leadership paradigm. As you will see in the next chapter, the four polarity characteristics of leaders alone are insufficient to leading breakthrough change. The most obvious example is a leader with tremendous visionary capacity, a person years ahead of his or her time. Let us consider Reverend Dr. Martin Luther King Jr. If Dr. King were to only speak to the vision embodied in his "I Have a Dream" speech and failed to acknowledge the present state, he would have assumed less credibility, perhaps even been accused of having his head in the clouds. His strength was in his ability to envision a powerful future while at the same time being connected to, and grounded in, the current state of race relations.

SUMMARY LEARNINGS

1. By *manager,* we mean the individual who maintains control of a system and/or subsystem of the organization. A manager may or may not have other people working for him or her.

2. The four characteristics of the great manager are: administrative, energetic, analytical, and performer—however, these characteristics alone are insufficient to lead transformational change.

TO ACTION

1. From the perspective of self, what are your strengths and learning opportunities with respect to the four managerial characteristics?

2. From the point of view of your relationships at work, how can you better administer your relationships to produce desired results?

3. Where do you derive your current energy flow? What might you change to improve upon the source?

4. In considering your enterprise, are your managers focused on achieving the organization's mission and vision? What plan might you put in place to refocus your managers on the organization's endeavor?

ENDNOTES

1. Abraham Zaleznik, "Managers and Leaders: Are They Different?" *Harvard Business Review, A Collection of Articles: Best of HBR on Leadership: Balancing Stability and Change* (Boston, MA: Harvard Business School Publishing, Product Number 8288, 2001): 7.
2. John Kotter, "What Leaders Really Do," *Harvard Business Review, A Collection of Articles: Best of HBR on Leadership: Balancing Stability and Change* (Product Number 8288, 2001): 24.
3. Ibid, 27.
4. John Kotter, "What Leaders Really Do," *Harvard Business Review, A Collection of Articles: Best of HBR on Leadership: Balancing Stability and Change* (Boston, MA: Harvard Business School Publishing, Product Number 8288, 2001): 27.
5. Stephen Hacker, Marta Wilson, and Cindy Johnston, *Work Miracles* (Blacksburg, VA: Insight Press, 1999): 49.
6. John Kotter, "What Effective General Managers Really Do," *Harvard Business Review, A Collection of Articles: Best of HBR on Leadership: Balancing Stability and Change* (Boston, MA: Harvard Business School Publishing, Product Number 8288, 2001): 43.

6

What Makes a
Great Leader?

First, a few words about leadership and management. As discussed in chapter 4, leadership and management are different. Historically, people who have assumed these roles were different individuals with radically different characteristics. It's no surprise that when we think about the characteristics of leaders, we turn to the descriptors of visionary, creative, and empowering. When we describe managers, we say they are pragmatic, energetic, analytical, and our star performers. We know that top leadership teams or a chief executive sets the vision and direction of an organization. Managers are called upon to take that vision and establish a predictable plan for achieving it, while at the same time administering the base business. As a matter of routine, the manager is asked to target a system or subsystem for incremental improvement.

Two top leaders today are required to radically rethink their organizations frequently simply to survive, let alone thrive. Transition to an organization of meaning offers hope for new or renewed organizations to flourish in today's competitive marketplace and rapid change. In this vein, higher competency to lead transformational change must be sought. In his article "What Leaders Really Do," John Kotter states:

> Leadership and management are two distinctive and complementary systems of action. Each has its own function and characteristic activities. Both are necessary for success in an increasingly complex and volatile business environment. Most U.S. corporations are over-managed and under-led. They need to develop their capacity to exercise leadership.[1]

Corporations, small and large, are hungry for leadership. Clearly it is the formal role of top leadership to lead the transformation of the organization.

However, creating and nurturing change agents within the organization is also vital to long-term success.

As such, we evolve the term *leader-manager,* where managers are also called upon to support breakthrough change efforts. Drawing upon the strengths of their managerial skills, managers would benefit by developing their strengths and capacities in the leadership characteristics, which is easier said than done. As you will see, the leadership characteristics are polar opposites of the managerial characteristic set.

There are thousands of leadership books that speak to the various qualities and skills required to lead change. Every year, hundreds more are placed on the shelves of bookstores around the world. Some of these texts are based on the lifetime experiences of a single leader, in a sense, an autobiography of the lessons reaped during their individual experience. While valuable and often interesting, these texts are based on a single perspective or experience. Other books expand their perspective to include a number of important leaders seeking to identify common leadership characteristics, again drawing important lessons in leadership. Finally, some books take a more academic or consulting approach through the study of the body of knowledge in leadership and identification of leadership principles, methods, and tools.

Our unique view of what makes a great leader is one that includes a wide review of the literature on leadership while attempting to synthesize the knowledge into key areas of focus. Since our goal is breakthrough change, we include those predominate characteristics embodied in leaders who have successfully transformed their enterprise, producing radically different, positive results (see Figure 6.1).

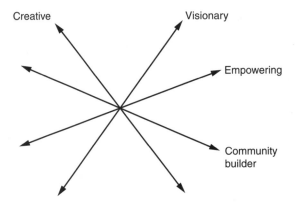

Figure 6.1   Characteristics of the leadership domain.

The leadership characteristics are also redefined as observed in the *conscious* leader. For example, *empowerment* is traditionally defined as providing employees with the authority, responsibility, *and* accountability for specific business systems, goals, or tasks.[2] This is a highly effective definition that provides a framework for thinking through the dynamics of transferring over time greater amounts of responsibility and decision making throughout the organization, and it can be particularly helpful in transition to an organization of meaning. However, we also offer another view on empowerment, one that is particularly relevant to leading an organization of meaning. We define *empowerment* as *aiding in the discovery of power found within others for their life purpose.* In the organization described in chapter 3, the transformational leader's role in empowering others actually transcends the creation of defined boundaries and conversion of power to employees. In an organization of meaning, transformational leaders are called upon to help others access the power *from within themselves* through clarity of purpose and self-awareness and to manifest that power through their unique talents and gifts. In this way, power is no longer conferred upon another but enlisted, drawn from the spirit.

COMMUNITY-BUILDING

If you were the spiritual and political leader of more than six million people and were kicked out of your country by a foreign power, how would you maintain and even grow your community? This is the challenge that faces the Dalai Lama. Part of the Dalai Lama's skill in building community is the manner in which he avoids the typical categorization of people. Normally, people are placed in the *for me, neutral,* or *against me* categories. This classification begins to limit those within our community and the possibilities for partnerships, learning opportunities, and indeed, friendships. There is value to our knowledge-gaining capability by entertaining a slightly different view of our enemies. The Dalai Lama states:

> When we are faced with an enemy, a person or group of people wishing us harm, we can view this as an opportunity to develop patience and tolerance. We need these qualities: they are useful to us. And the only occasion we have to develop them is when we are challenged by an enemy. So, from this point of view, our enemy is our guru, our teacher. Irrespective of their motivations, from our point of view, enemies are very beneficial, a blessing.[3]

People may not really understand their enemies, simply basing their thoughts upon single impressions. According to the Dalai Lama:

Friend and enemy are defined in terms of people's attitudes toward us and their treatment of us. Those whom we believe to have affection for us, to love and care for us, we generally regard as friends and loved ones. Those whom we believe to have ill will and harmful intentions toward us are our enemies. We therefore view people as friends or enemies based upon our perception of the thoughts and emotions they harbor toward us. So, nobody is essentially our friend or essentially our enemy.[4]

Effective community-building requires holding an abundance mentality that is energy embracing and inclusive. Living in this mind-set opens up a universe of opportunity. Different from competition, which if left unchecked can result in an unproductive and narrow mind-set of scarcity, abundance thinking transcends individual concern and promotes community. Through a community-based model, all players are strengthened and reap rewards. Ben Zander and Rosamund Stone Zander state in *The Art of Possibility:*

> Let's suppose that a universe of possibility stretches beyond the world of measurement to include all worlds: infinite, generative and abundant. Unimpeded on a daily basis by the concern for survival, free from the generalized assumption of scarcity, a person stands in the great space of possibility in a posture of openness, with an unfettered imagination for what can be.[5]

So at the start, when considering community, hold open the possibility of all persons and groups as potential community members where alliances formed from common interests and values can be beneficial. This is not to say all persons or groups have common interests or shared values, but rather by suspending our assumptions just for the moment, followed by a deeper review, one may discover that a person or group can be embraced within a broader community context. Great community builders seek the shifts in people and groups over time and build unique, unconventional unions. They see that the world of opportunity is vast, allowing for all in the community to flourish.

VISIONING

Top performers in visioning understand that painting the picture of the future is but part of the equation. Equally important is the reason to move toward a new horizon. If we were to paint a picture of a wonderful gourmet meal, the appeal would come from your association with complementary smells, tastes, and feelings of satisfied hunger. Think about it: lobster dripping with butter, a double-baked potato accompanied with fresh asparagus and a chocolate torte for dessert. Or maybe you prefer a steak with all the trimmings including a draft beer. But the vision of such a succulent meal does not stand alone. The appeal in large part rests upon your current state of hunger. In a setting where hunger is the current state, the promise of the gourmet meal vision is enticing and compelling. The reason to move toward the vision of the meal is found in your stomach.

But in another setting, for instance, having just finished a feast where you could not see consuming any more food, not even a small chocolate wafer, the mention of a gourmet meal is repulsive. The vision of the meal has not changed; yet, the state of your current condition and mind-set does not wish to move toward the vision. Therefore, speaking more about the vision and working to persuade you toward the meal would be a waste of effort.

Let's look at an expert leader in the art of visioning. His ability to paint a picture of harmony and peaceful coexistence of all of humanity with flowing words and imagery is renowned. Reverend Dr. Martin Luther King Jr. is often quoted from his "I Have a Dream" speech of 1964 on the Lincoln Memorial steps in Washington, D.C. The address is one of the most memorable of the last century and clearly outlined his desired future state:

> When we let freedom ring, when we let it ring from every village and every hamlet, from every state and every city, we will be able to speed up that day when all of God's children, black men and white men, Jews and Gentiles, Protestants and Catholics, will be able to join hands and sing in the words of the old Negro spiritual, "Free at last! Free at last! Thank God Almighty, we are free at last!"[6]

But equally significant was the complementary concept of why staying in the same post-Civil War state, largely defined by Jim Crow laws, was not an option. King, in his book *Why We Can't Wait*, outlines the argument for action, albeit nonviolent action. He speaks to the tendency to stay put, not to embark on the civil rights revolution as not being an option given the current realities. The word *wait* has an insidious, hidden meaning of *never* as it is applied against the struggle for civil rights. King declared, "Oppressed people cannot remain oppressed forever. The yearning for freedom eventually manifests itself, and that is what has happened to the American Negro."[7]

In the current business world, imagining a culture of excellent quality as represented by Six Sigma is often in the minds of leadership. Part of the challenge is seeing what such a quality program can deliver to performance. But as a leader, conveying this image to others is critical. Right away, language becomes a barrier. Once a program or approach is shared, all sorts of descriptors are introduced, creating a defensive posture in the organization. If, however, the burning platform of the organization's current state is effectively communicated (for example, poor sales, negative business impact due to deficient quality, reductions in workforce), the new program is born out of a perceived need. Resistance is lowered. The language and the ideas of Six Sigma are readily accepted.

EMPOWERING

Successful sharing of the compelling vision held by the leader fertilizes the soil from which empowerment can take root in others and be sustained over time. Historically, the role of a great leader was to get the troops in line and headed in the direction of the organization's vision. This command and control leadership approach, while still valid in few circumstances, falls far short of what is needed in today's environment. The new role of a leader is to discover the power naturally found within others and to direct it toward the vision of the enterprise. This power lies within each of us, a power that is increasingly heightened through deeper clarity of life purpose, vision, and goals (see Figure 6.2).

In our experience, empowerment is a natural and desirable outcome of building an organization of conscious individuals living out their life purpose as connected to the organization's mission, vision, and goals. Gaining mastery in empowering others often requires the leader to rethink the historical separation of vocation from the rest of life. It requires the leader to relate to the whole person, not just the job he or she was hired to perform. Helping individuals to discover their life's purpose and how this is connected to their work is a new concept for many, but it is a key ingredient to empowerment. Leaders are required to understand the unique dreams and talents of their employees to achieve mastery in empowerment.

Leaders today are called upon to be coaches, acting as a stand for the greatness of others within the enterprise. They seek to understand the whole person, his or her purpose, desires, and interests and look for the individual's vector of energy for the organization's vision, free of manipulation. This doesn't mean that the leader compromises the needs of the organization when a match is not identified, but he or she honors the individual. Most often when the vector of energy is not apparent, a healthy separation occurs.

Empowered individuals see themselves in the organization's vision. They hold a personal and strong desire to see that vision become a reality. Beyond monetary reward or stability, it is rather an expression of spirit and fulfilled life vision. When building an enterprise where all are conscious of life purpose, the problem of external motivation becomes secondary, perceived as an opportunity to appreciate others for their contribution as opposed to an incentive for action.

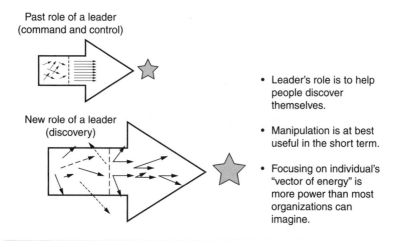

Past role of a leader
(command and control)

- Leader's role is to help people discover themselves.

New role of a leader
(discovery)

- Manipulation is at best useful in the short term.

- Focusing on individual's "vector of energy" is more power than most organizations can imagine.

Figure 6.2 Alignment of individual vectors of energy (small arrows) toward an organization's vision (stars).

CREATIVITY

Robert Fritz holds the view that "there is a deep longing to create that resides within the soul of humanity.[8] In our view, creativity is the expression of individual or collective spirit manifest in the world. Embodied in all human experience is the potential for creativity; all people are born with this gift. Just take a look at a small child alone or at play with another. They have an extraordinary capacity to create compared to many adults. They are creating ideas, games, and imaginary adventures and friends all the time. Unfortunately, as children grow older, this expression of creativity is stifled. *Play,* which we define as *vigor in exploration,* is an experience or luxury adults tap only for weekend hobbies.

Until recently, problem solving—using intellect to fix the immediate problems at hand—has dominated our economic system. Today, creativity is a rapidly growing demand of the workforce. As we saw earlier, employees possess a growing desire to contribute their creativity, passion, or spirit in the workplace with the best and the brightest seeking to work for enterprises that promote and value their ideas and interests.

Creativity requires purpose, imagination, curiosity, and courage, bringing back a childlike nature of wonder and awe. While problem solving, becoming overly reliant on critical thinking skills thwarts curiosity and imagination. Problem solving is a mind-set of fixing or making something go away. Creativity is the mind-set of creation or bringing something new into existence.

Creativity is sourced from spirit, a personal passion to bring something new into the world. Transformational leaders must possess a clear life purpose and the ability to coach others in the discovery of their life purpose. With this clarity in place at the individual and collective levels, the path to creativity is made wide for many more to travel.

Michael Ray and Rochelle Myers use the word *essence* to describe one's inner creative potential and resource.[9] This essence provides the quality of intuition, will, joy, strength, and compassion at the heart of a person's creative base. When engaged in creativity, it is important to bring consciousness to the nature of being instead of having and doing. Consciousness of life purpose, meditation, and conversation about one's values and aspirations all grant admission to the unique nature of one's own being. Creativity also requires you to remain detached from expectations, so that you can broaden your thoughts and ideas.

Creativity at the collective level can be limited or expanded by an organization's view or preconceptions about *who* will be creative, *what* they will do, and *when* and *how* they will do it.[10] Transformational leaders are able to give up their preconceptions about who, what, when, and how. Rather, they openly and graciously hold a worldview that all human beings possess a unique creative essence that can and should be resourced.

Great leaders acknowledge the problem presented and rather than diving directly into it, take two or even ten steps forward for an expanded view. Hence, the exploration of disparate ideas, reframing, and opportunity generation begins. Through the creative process, great leaders transcend a problem while, at the same time, addressing it magically. The leader's personal passion for the idea stimulates the creative process and is a source of courage to move ahead boldly.

SELF, INTERPERSONAL, AND ENTERPRISE MASTERY

Consider the four leadership characteristics in the context of personal, interpersonal, and enterprise mastery. Chapter 8 provides a powerful tool for gaining deeper clarity of life direction. For example, at the level of the individual, or self mastery, ask yourself, "What is the vision for my life? Where am I overly reliant on my analytical skills and missing creative opportunities to express my purpose in life?"

In the arena of relationship, where are you *not* generating a vision for the relationship? Where are you building community and seeking to form shared goals with the people in your life?

With respect to the endeavor of your organization, do you have a vision for the organization? Can you successfully attract others internally and externally to help you advance your vision? Why do your employees come to work every day? Are they connected to the endeavor, or are they just putting in time? Do you know? What arena of leadership—visioning, empowering, community building, or creativity—would be a key leverage area of improvement for you in leading the organization?

Understanding your capacities in the areas of leadership at the level of self-mastery, relational mastery, and enterprise mastery is important to becoming an effective transformational leader.

NOT EITHER/OR, RATHER MANAGEMENT *AND* LEADERSHIP

Organizations are filled with persons with diverse skill sets. In some cases, people demonstrate strong managerial skills, but the required transformational leadership skills are not in abundance. What is tragic is the promotion of persons because of strong managerial skills without a prior assessment of the needed leadership skills. This is a prescription for failure.

When understanding the differences between managerial skills and leadership skills, the door is open for improved performance with regards to personnel management. The use of technical development paths, in addition to leadership development paths, has been introduced into several organizations. Also, the identification of potential leaders has been utilized. But the most promising aspect of performance enhancement has fallen short of its promise—building upon the diversity of the organization. When an organization can identify the skill strengths of its members and develop the required alignment and supportive approach, it can see an explosion of results delivery.

TRANSFORMATIONAL LEADERSHIP

Transformational leadership embodies all eight characteristics or traits embraced in the management and leadership sciences (see Figure 6.3).

Transformational leadership calls upon the leader to be capable of envisioning a new future (what can be) while at the same time being analytical about the current reality (what is today). The transformational leader employs and fosters creative thinking (outside the box) while being proficient in the administration of the business (inside the box). He or she is

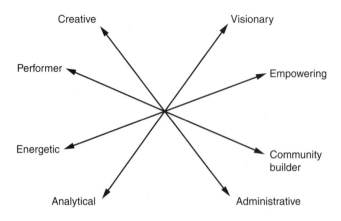

Figure 6.3   All eight traits of transformational leadership.

energetic (power within) and knows how to empower others (tapping power in others). Finally, the transformational leader is a results producer and knows how to build community to attain results through many.

PULLING TRANSFORMATIONAL LEADERSHIP TOGETHER

Throughout this book, we have talked about the components of transformational leadership. At the core of transformational leadership is consciousness at the level of self, relationships, and the enterprise, a challenging task in itself. Fortunately, producing higher levels of consciousness within the individual and the group is a key leverage area for producing transformation, so the work with self and in relation to others is often worth the effort. Being part of a purposeful organization of meaning is a life-giving, joyous experience for all.

Transformational leaders must also hold an internal and external focus, seeking to understand the internal dynamics of the organization while simultaneously attending to external forces and a broader community of people holding the organization's license to live. Understanding the value of standardization and change to the organization and the tension that can arise between the two is also a requirement of the transformational leader. Finally, transformational leaders must possess not one set of skills over another but both managerial and leadership skills (see Figure 6.4).

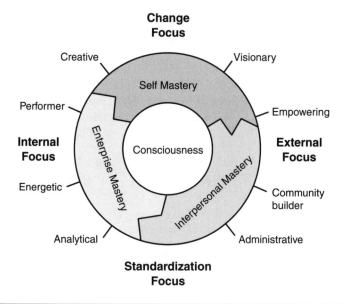

Figure 6.4   Transformational leadership model.

SUMMARY LEARNINGS

1. There exist four primary characteristics of leadership.

2. These characteristics alone are insufficient to lead transformational change.

3. These four characteristics combined with the four managerial characteristics are required to lead transformational change.

4. The transformational leadership model allows us to see these differences as they apply to different aspects of the organization.

TO ACTION

1. Do you have a personal vision for your life?

2. Do you have a vision for your organization? Are you able to articulate the need for change?

3. What steps are you taking to enlist the support for your vision of people within and outside of your organization?

4. What is your overall strategy for alignment and attunement of your organization?

5. Have you established barriers to expressions of spirit or creativity in your organization? What can you do to remove those barriers?

ENDNOTES

1. John Kotter, "What Leaders Really Do," *Best of Harvard Business Review, A Collection of Articles* (Boston, MA: Harvard Business School Publishing, Product Number 8288, 2001): 23.
2. Marsha Willard, presentation to participants of the Change Agent Training and Leadership Strategies Program, September 2002.
3. Dalai Lama, *An Open Heart: Practicing Compassion in Everyday Life*, Edited by Nicholas Vreeland (Boston: Little, Brown and Company, 2001): 21.
4. Ibid, 112.
5. Rosamund Stone-Zander and Ben Zander, *The Art of Possibility* (Harvard Business School Press, 2000): 19.
6. http://www.mlkonline.com/
7. Martin Luther King Jr., *Why We Can't Wait* (New York: New American Library, 2000): 76.
8. Robert Fritz, *Creating* (New York: Random House, 1981): 3.
9. Michael Ray and Rochelle Myers, *Creativity in Business* (New York: Doubleday Dell, 1986): 8.
10. Alan Robinson and Sam Stern, *Corporate Creativity: How Innovation and Improvement Actually Happen* (San Francisco: Berrett-Koehler, 1997): 20.

LEADERSHIP VIGNETTE

Larry Norvell

Leadership Position: CEO

Organization: United Way of the Columbia Willamette, Portland, Oregon

Transformational Results: Historically, the United Way of the Columbia Willamette, like many other service organizations, held a vision that was primarily focused on raising a threshold of money to fund its list of programs. More than two years ago, Larry passionately articulated a new vision for the organization—a vision that focuses on the actual impact that United Way can have on the quality of human lives. His vision—to have an impact on more than 100,000 lives in the Portland and Vancouver metro areas—has produced a different mind-set within the organization, a mind-set that has extended to community partners. The new mind-set is one of collaboration and deeper community connection. More creativity has resulted with staff and partners looking beyond financial resources, to identify other resources that can be brought to bear to change the lives of clients. The vision has rallied a broader group of people to work together to impact the lives of Portland and Vancouver residents who benefit from the programs of United Way. The organization has increased its ability and clarity in measuring outcomes, opposed to activities. Within the next two years, the organization will be able to share hard, measurable facts about the impact United Way has had on the lives of the people it serves, making it possible for people to know that their contributions actually have an impact.

Reflections on Transformation[1]

What learnings do you have on creating a burning platform for change?

If you are going to make significant change, the leader must be grounded in reality as well as hold a vision. In my view, that reality must be almost painful, as the pain helps to propel you forward. You can have a dream, but if the current reality is simply fine, you may not find the energy to go for the vision. If the platform is on fire, such as rapid revenue decline and possible closure of business, people within the organization will want to get out of the current dilemma.

We had to ask ourselves "so what" if the United Way of the Columbia Willamette were no longer. We discovered that we mattered, that many people in our community would not receive vital services if we closed our doors.

I argue that the best thing for business today is the tough economy. These times will require organizations to think more deeply about their reason for being, to reflect on their vision and core values, and to make significant change in their organization. In my organization, we cut our operating budget 15 percent and decreased staff 15 percent this year, both tough undertakings, but today we are a more focused, more efficient, and more effective organization. That probably would not have happened if we did not have the tough economy.

What were your learnings on personal transformation as part of organizational transformation?

A leader has to be clear on what he or she is hoping to accomplish and, again, attuned to current reality. If you are not clear or grounded in reality, you simply won't be as successful. Also, if you can't turn yourself around, it will be uphill trying to turn around an organization. I have had to change as much as a person as the organization has had to change.

What about personal transformation of others?

People who are willing to take a look at their own life situation and give some thought to what they aspire to accomplish in life can transform. It requires soul searching and reflection to see if there exists incongruence between the current reality and one's aspirations. Any gap between what one aspires to create and the current reality can leave one unsettled, desiring to change. In my experience, it requires some unhappiness with current reality, as the tension between what's so and what's possible will pull you forward.

How did you reach out beyond United Way and have other people join you in the vision?

We proactively reached out to people we hoped would be a part of our vision, talking with CEOs of major companies, local foundations, and providers. We built an ideal matrix of people and groups that we would need to move our vision for the community forward. We discovered lots of consistency in terms of what we all aspired to do. I found that what we have in common with others far exceeds what we don't have in common. We tapped our common aspirations to come up with strategies to accomplish our shared goals.

ENDNOTE

1. Transcript excerpts, interview with Larry Norvell, March 27, 2003, Portland, Oregon, conducted by Tammy Roberts.

7

When Great Managers Fail to Become Great Leaders

Evolving to an organization of meaning requires leadership beyond the top executive. Putting the right people in leadership positions within the organization will accelerate your transformation journey. Building transformational leadership talent within your organization is imperative.

Historically, organizations have promoted their best managers to leadership without validation that the manager possesses the leadership qualities needed to do the job. This chapter focuses on this key pitfall in the traditional approach to promotion, offering strategies for change in how to identify new leaders.

LOST OPPORTUNITIES

For example, Sue was viewed as an upcoming star. Bright, aggressive and willing to put forth the required effort, she was a favorite. Having graduated from a top-tier engineering school, the transition into the working world of a large environmental engineering firm seemed flawless. Performance feedback sessions concentrated on her ability to work within the system and to achieve the personal targeted work goals. After nearly three years of stellar performance, stepping up to a supervising role in the central office was regarded as the next logical step. Following this assignment as supervisor for a couple of years, Sue was destined to lead a small field office. All was well.

But from the time of the promotion announcement, the golden-paved road started to show potholes. Her team to lead contained a jealous coworker, Gene, who believed he should have been given the assignment. As the weeks moved forward, Gene positioned himself as an obstacle to the team's success. In addition, the project to be accomplished by the team appeared daunting to Sue. She did not feel technically competent in every aspect of the project nor feel confident in guiding the project through several known regulatory barriers. Holding her doubts inside in order not to look weak, Sue worried intensely. The team looked for direction. Sue retreated inward, plagued by indecision.

Management worked to guide her, and with failure becoming a real possibility, these coaching engagements did not produce much. Frustration ruled. Why did such a promising superstar stumble in the transition to leadership? Why, with strong personal contribution skills, did Sue not simply notch her gun with another success? The system saw the challenge to leadership as a linear progression from great management performance, but in fact, it was a new course of study.

A similar story can be told in many organizations. Carol Walker has also seen this promotional issue at work. She has seen the failure of new leaders who were promoted primarily for technical competence. Technical competence often fails to translate into meaningful team leadership. In the article "Saving Your Rookie Managers from Themselves," as a coach and consultant, she observed dysfunctional, newly promoted managers.[1] She notes five problem areas of rookie managers: delegating, getting support from senior staffers, projecting confidence, thinking strategically, and giving feedback.

Compounding the problem in acquiring new skills, the rookie manager often becomes insecure and self-focused. This causes a hesitation to ask for help and a lack of active support for the team. The team loses trust, and a gap occurs in effective leadership.

Lost opportunities for individuals selected to make the transition to leadership and for the organization can be avoided. The transition to leadership from individual contributor is fraught with difficulties. What is there to learn, and more importantly, how can an organization increase its successes?

THE UNIQUE CONTRIBUTION
OF LEADERSHIP

As laid out in previous chapters, leadership is distinctly different from management. Management skills are necessary to the organization's operation but do not necessarily translate into great leadership. The movement toward leadership from strong management is anything but linear. Community building, visioning, creating, and empowering are the polar opposites of the management skills performing (self), analyzing, administrating, and self-energizing.

Children and maturing young people experience these differences. Individual sports such as tennis, swimming, or running require self-discipline, following the rules, and individual skill development. But contrasted with team sports such as soccer, softball, and basketball, a new set of skills must be learned—team skills. Furthermore, given leadership roles within teams, additional challenges present themselves. The challenge of leading an interdependent group of players appears. No longer is an individual's skill level of chief importance. For the team leader is concerned about the whole, the performance of each individual, and the team as a whole. Simple lessons learned, but what happened to this knowledge in the adult world of organizational effectiveness?

In the adult working world, people seemed to have forgotten many of these lessons. It is like taking the best player and making him or her team captain. The transition to leadership is often left to fate, lacking proper preparation and training. And the persons picked to make this leap of chance are often the ones displaying high competence in polar opposite skills. No wonder failure is delivered to the doorstep.

Often the reason behind choosing the best performer on a team and making him or her team leader is for reward purposes. By moving up the food chain of the organization's infrastructure, more dollars and benefits are granted. Great for the recognition of good work, but a crapshoot on obtaining strong leadership in the days ahead. And the gamble is not only one for the organization; it is a gamble on the team member. The risk is that the person displaying these great managerial skills will fail. Once a system has experienced the risk and subsequent level of failure using the promotion for managerial merit approach, the conflict of objectives (reward, leadership development) produces a bizarre condition. Some high performers, fearing the reward of promotion, will back off in performance and keep a low profile. The system we have produced eliminates this problem.

A straightforward correction to this nonsensical leadership selection process (promotion based solely on rewarding managerial skills) has been made by several organizations. By using multiple career paths, rewards can be tailored to match increased performance. A great engineer receives the rewards of increased pay and benefits without the move to a leadership position and is granted the title of senior engineer with broader project responsibilities. A contribution-based reward system further adds logic into the decision making. A contribution-based pay system focuses on the actual performance of the individual. It moves rewards beyond time on a job or skill level alone to an actual contribution to the health of the organization.

For instance, a great manufacturing line operator moves ahead in terms of pay based upon contribution in the current role. Seniority and demonstrated skills may play minor roles, but actual performance is paramount in the reward system. Therefore, the line operator can realize rewards in the current role without having to transfer or get promoted to make more money and achieve recognition.

By recognizing the unique contribution of the leader and broadening the reward and career systems, an organization can avoid many pitfalls. The organization can have its cake and eat it too—great leaders, great team members, and rewards for performance.

LEADERSHIP SKILL DEVELOPMENT

Leadership development may have become the Holy Grail for some organizations by building up leadership capacities. Recognizing the importance of leadership is healthy. But sometimes the methods for developing leadership appear a bit strange. *The Houston Chronicle* (as reported by *Parade Magazine,* December 30, 2001) presented one such example:

> At a motivational seminar designed to improve employee bonding, 10 Burger King executives suffered first- and second-degree burns while walking barefoot on burning charcoal. "The first two steps were all right," said Kim Miller, director of marketing for Burger King. "Then, of course, it got hotter. I was test-marketing our newest sandwich—fillet of sole."

Ropes courses, trust walks, mountain climbing, rafting challenges, outdoor survival courses, Zen meditation, leadership guru-of-the-month coaching sessions, primal grunting are all available for your exploration.

These methods may be productive given certain contexts, but there are three general approaches we wish to put forth.

Avoid an Abrupt Transition to Leadership

In other words, further leadership skill development early in the process so the movement from management to leadership is not whiplash inducing. Offer a consistent, holistic model of leadership to the whole organization. Broadly communicate the leadership skill set required. The organization can begin to better understand the essential leadership skill, the importance of managerial skills, and the difference between the two. Obviously, we would recommend the leadership model from this text. But, more important than one particular model, *a* model needs to be presented. Having the organization guess about the leadership skills deemed important is not productive. Pick a leadership model, narrow down precise definitions within the model, promote the leadership skills, and draw attention to the application of the skills.

Also, give leadership opportunities to managers without making a full-fledged promotion to a full-time leadership position. Special assignments that advance leadership skill development are advised. Be it a special task force or a standing part-time role as a leader, give people a chance to learn, experiment, and develop.

Identify Persons with Predisposition toward Leadership

As evidenced by past experience and competency in the leadership skills outlined, seek out employees who already demonstrate informal leadership. For new hires, move the employment or membership evaluation process to include leadership skills assessment.

Within an identified group of potential leaders, give leadership skill assessments to determine strengths and improvement opportunities. With this information, a leadership development plan can be developed. Assignments to nurture and strengthen skills and to address improvement opportunities can now be arranged.

Caution needs to be given with concern to this identification recommendation. The objective is to identify natural leaders, persons who already display the leadership skill set. It is not to create a category for favored sons or daughters. Some organizations have overemphasized the leaders in development grouping and elevated their status to golden boys and girls. Resentment grows among the nonselected, and the selected begin to exhibit an entitlement posture. The counterapproach is not to select in secret; instead, the importance of management within the organizational culture is the offset. If management of important systems is considered a lesser role to leadership in general, then the ranks of leadership will carry a blessed status. Make management important in word, deed, and recognition; position leadership as an important but different skill set.

Identify Persons with the Desire to Be Leaders

Having the organization identify potential leaders is but one part of the equation. It is not uncommon to find persons who can lead, but do not want to lead. Simply identifying leaders and making assignments may force talent to exit by choice, not wanting to play the leadership role. Likewise, some people with little in the way of visible leadership may have a real passion to lead. When a balanced system exists that values both management and leadership, the best way of discovering the leadership desire is to ask. Career mapping, in dialog, offers tremendous opportunity for conscious development for both parties. So sit down with people and ask where their passion lies, what is their heart's desire, and its origin. Promises and commitments do not necessarily need to be an outcome. Having the knowledge itself is significant.

HIRING FOR LEADERSHIP

Ideally, leadership assessment starts at the hiring process. One way to stack the deck in terms of obtaining dynamic leadership is to select leaders at the beginning of the process. The search evolves around persons having displayed significant levels of the required leadership skills in past experiences. Interview questions, hiring evaluations, and position descriptions speak in some manner toward leadership.

The quest for leadership skills in the hiring process does not guarantee that all hires will be superb leaders. Some persons will find the management of systems to be a more satisfying course once in the door, and others will choose the leadership course. But seeking persons with leadership in the beginning offers a way to bias the pool to the leadership alternative, presenting a larger cluster of future leaders.

Initial assignments should have a leadership component. In this way, sharpening leadership skills within the context of the tasks to be accomplished is the challenge—not relying upon a cathartic conversion by every soul to leadership excellence.

Leadership assessment at the time of hiring is found in a small but growing number of organizations. The prevalent practice is to hire for the immediate need, hoping that some leaders will have been caught up in the hiring net to be used at a later time. No wonder leadership deficiencies are found in organizations. The trouble lies in the hiring procedures utilized. The hiring process focuses on a short-term objective of fulfilling a particular position or acquiring labor for a job category. The long-term skill requirement of transformational leadership is not adequately addressed. The immediate need drives the interview, which results in technical skill application and work history directly related to a particular vacancy, but what about the future requirements?

Organizations that are moving to fuller assessments, which consider leadership skill, are reaping the benefits by attracting more leaders to run the current business and future leaders for expansion. And there is another aspect to this broader view. Given that the organization's longer planning horizon is evident in the hiring process, the employee is influenced from the beginning to adopt a career perspective. Turnover reductions are experienced.

BUILDING A LEADERSHIP ORGANIZATION

There is a special kind of organization, one that has leadership responsibilities throughout all positions. Within these organizations, leadership is a base requirement. A leadership organization is one in which leadership permeates every layer, every position grouping. It is not necessarily utopia for all. Whether or not a leadership-heavy organization is right is dependant upon the business needs, the work to be accomplished, the organizational value exchange with its customers, and the goods or services being provided. For instance, a fast food outlet does not call for the considerable investment of a leadership organization, whereas an integrated manufacturing site may.

A transformation of the entire organization with regard to leadership is possible. The potential is leadership in abundance. Imagine having strong, effective leadership skills in every corner, in every situation, and in every gathering. How could such a system come into being?

Broad leadership can be, and has been, produced within organizations. Our collective experiences in both leading and consulting with world-class organizations verifies that leadership organizations do exist and outperform the traditional top-down, controlling model, given their appropriate usage. The description and embedded ideas of a leadership organization are often found to be alluring to many. But despite its attractiveness, creating a leadership organization is often met with failure. It is in the work and philosophy changes needed to produce such organizations where failure to make broad leadership a reality exists. It is easy to espouse the virtues of *people first* and *people are our primary asset.* But to create a leadership organization, the actions, beliefs, and words must match. Words without corresponding actions reveal nonsupportive beliefs and counterproductive behavior. We submit five key steps to creating a leadership organization:

1. *Seek in the beginning.* Select for leadership skills in all positions during the hiring process. Hiring for the long-term leadership requirements is a smart way of raising the input quality into the leadership organization.

2. *Evaluate performance.* Make leadership part of the performance feedback process for all employees. Communicate from the beginning the leadership skills desired and evaluate the individual's performance against this skill set. Have people fashion an improvement plan and tailor career plans to build leadership abilities.

3. *Standardize approach.* Select a leadership model, language, and approach. Don't cause useless confusion by seizing upon the leadership

model of the month. Although not all leadership models or approaches produce quality leaders for today's organization, there are many good and solid ones to choose from. Pick one and standardize.

   4. *Reward performance.* Reward leadership performance. Individuals displaying the desired leadership skills need to be rewarded. And since a leadership organization sets a base requirement for leadership, people who cannot or choose not to display leadership must find another playing field for their energies. Counseling nonperformers out of the organization is part of creating a leadership organization. Root causes for how such a person was hired to begin with must be identified and corrected. Many times a poor fit of interests and skills was made in the hiring process, a costly and unproductive system fault.

   5. *Remove hierarchy.* Flatten the organization by removing layers and increasing the span of responsibility. Give all persons the opportunity to lead. Remove hierarchy as the sole determinant of who leads teams or initiatives. Spread the leadership responsibilities.

   A holistic approach must be taken in creating this leadership organization. And when looking at the whole system, the input is critical. What is the selection criteria used in bringing on new employees? Does a common, well-understood leadership model exist? What performance process is in place to prompt leadership development? And does the reward system support the intent of the performance feedback? Does everyone have plentiful opportunities to lead? A leadership organization answers these questions with solid, well-defined systems that promote leadership.

SUMMARY LEARNINGS

1. Rewarding managerial competencies with promotion to leadership is risky due to the differing skill requirements.

2. Dual track promotion systems, which recognize managerial contributions and leadership aptitude separately, offer an alternative to management to leadership promotion alone.

3. In developing leadership, avoid the abrupt transition from managing systems to leading people; identify people with leadership skills and identify people interested in leadership roles.

4. Hiring people based on the long-term view of leadership requirements versus hiring for the immediate need is a step in creating a leadership organization.

5. A unique type of leadership organization exists where all persons are charged with leadership responsibilities.

TO ACTION

1. Reflecting on your current hiring system, how would you change it to identify and develop emerging leaders in your organization?

2. Who in your organization was promoted to leadership but lacks the leadership traits needed to advance your transformation initiative? What can you do to support them?

ENDNOTE

1. Carlo A. Walker, "Saving Your Rookie Managers from Themselves," *Harvard Business Review* 80, no. 4 (2002): 97.

LEADERSHIP VIGNETTE

Norman Moleboge

Leadership Position: Police Commissioner

Organization: Botswana Police Service

Organizational Focus: Police Service for the Southern African Region country of Botswana, with a force of more than 6,500 uniformed officers, responsible for a civil population of 1.7 million citizens in a country roughly the size of Texas.

Transformational Results: Following time as a British protectorate, Botswana became a free and independent state in 1966. Since that time, the economy and welfare of its people has grown steadily, far outreaching the progress of its neighbors in terms of percentage growth, transparency, and governmental stability. As police commissioner, Norman Moleboge had produced what is considered unparalleled quality of service and respect for the police service. Recently, a new national and international police academy was built outside of Otse, Botswana, and is considered world-class in its training and progressive approach to maintaining civil order while enhancing community involvement.

Reflections on Transformation[1]

What was the approach you took in creating such a distinguished level of service and favorable community image in an area of the world where police have not normally been extended a high level of trust or respect?

First, I considered what amount of transformation I could put into place to achieve quality service delivery. Opportunities were already in place. My predecessor had started a program of restructuring, and I chose to carry on with this direction. This gave the chance for a better structure of human resources. Workload was better distributed, allowing people to better accomplish the work. It was one immediate plus for the change I was undertaking.

In addition, we created some symbolic changes such as informative items, rank structures, and new insignias. But we had to still address our core business—quality service. Our image in service delivery, both in image and reality, needed improvement.

We started on the journey with a detailed analysis. It was a taxing exercise, but we allowed everyone to have input. Leadership put itself in front of the staff and asked for a critique—what we were doing right, wrong, and what needed to change. I believed everything said, including things about the leadership. It was what people believed about us; there was no need to defend.

At this stage, our job was to come up with the programs to provide the needed changes. We started to source expertise inside and outside of the organization. We committed the needed programs to paper, consulting broadly in order to carry as many people as possible on board. This planning process took considerable time.

After having put programs into place, it was time to deliver. By consulting to such a broad extend and producing supporting guidelines and literature, we had few dissenting voices. There was no going back. We had to see that everyone delivered to their agreements. Although not at 100 percent, there were no major reservations about the programs to be undertaken.

And results have come forth. Our community image has completely changed to one of a competent and service-oriented organization. This was due to our impact on the crime rate and the way in which we conduct ourselves. We removed *police force* and moved to *police service.* This was recognized as truth versus a public relations ploy.

Service delivery results are supported not only by statistics but by accommodations from the public sector in the form of written testimonials in the press and letters sent directly to me.

What insights can you offer on implementation?

Pushing too many programs can overwhelm people with all the changes at one time. They may be willing, but the capacity comes into question. I have learned that you have to look at the magnitude of the changes to be undertaken. Do I do them all at once or will that saturate their capacity? When learning new processes, it is better to evaluate changes in small loads (increments). If changes have not achieved their targets, the leadership must forge ahead and correct. Change must be leader driven.

Slowing down a bit, interfacing changes with training programs can be beneficial. We had to introduce the major changes in installments through the ranks. We started with ourselves in headquarters, and then moved to departments. Three years were required for complete implementation, to completely cover the organization. Understand, we have people spread over a large geographical area with responsibility of total-country policing.

What where your learnings on personal transformation as part of organizational transformation?

My major motivation in opting for transformation was personal achievement and creation of a legacy for the Botswana Police Service. Why transformation? I saw myself over a period of 13 years from constable to deputy commissioner. And at that stage, I was one of the youngest deputy commissioners at age 33. After 15 years as a deputy, I ascended to the position of commissioner and saw this as one of the greatest opportunities available to change—to put into place transformational programs.

I was of the strong opinion that such opportunities were very great. No resentment existed within the service, as I had been promoted from within and not a stranger. My leadership was not in question. I wasn't concerned about job security, having already qualified for a pension.

But, did I have the necessary skills and resources to embark on these deep changes? My honest answer was that I did not have all the necessary expertise to bring about the change. But I believe the expertise was spread among the various members of the service. It was a matter of having each person recognize the areas of expertise he or she had and how to put these skills to use. I was prepared to learn new concepts and prepared to provide the leadership as it became clear to me what would be best for the service and for the country.

What about empowerment of your senior officers?

Empowerment. For my part, I made it a point to provide them with necessary training, responsibility, and authority.

Recently, we have effective major changes in our Police Act, in which my authority is to be shared down into the organization. The changes are almost through the civil approval process and close to implementation. I will be passing some of my powers down to my deputies, which will strengthen the service.

How did you reach out beyond Botswana and influence the southern African region?

I have had major involvement in effective regional policing in the southern African region. My first day as police commissioner (August 1, 1995), I was in Zimbabwe where we formed the Sub-African Regional Police Chiefs Cooperation (SARPCCO). Of 12 nations, I was the most junior of the police chiefs. Three years after its launch, I became its leader. I set the program in terms of what was to be achieved. The uniqueness about this organization is that it carries operations across boundaries, according to agreements ratified by governments. Joint operations are undertaken where countries go beyond just criminal intelligence. This is unusual, especially with countries where political disagreements are not uncommon. Police work continues where we may not necessarily agree with each other politically, but we have agreed on certain criminal matters. Also, for intelligence, Interpol has integrated with SARPCCO.

What is your vision for the Botswana Police Service 10 years out?

In all honesty, I foresee that the Botswana Police Service will take major steps in terms of additional changes in continued improving professionalism and in improving service delivery. And we have an effective measurement system to track our progress. In the Botswana community, we still have a major challenge to tackle. We have not brought the communities to fully appreciate their contribution in maintenance of law in their own communities.

ENDNOTE

1. Transcript excerpts, interview with Police Commissioner Norman S. Moleboge, February 4, 2003, Gaborone, Botswana, conducted by Stephen Hacker.

8

Building Blocks in Creating a Life of Meaning

Human beings have unlimited potential to create lives of accomplishment and personal fulfillment. However, a great number of people do not know where they are going in life. Gazing upon the stars at night, asking what life is all about, and contemplating individual purpose is a universal experience. Living through difficult times can produce the desire for meaning. And although it may be human nature to ask the question "Why am I here?" putting forth an answer is often the courageous step not taken. Why am I here? What purpose does my existence serve? What difference can I make with my life? Answering these questions is not an easy task. Creating a life of meaning requires patience, commitment, and time dedicated to personal mastery.

We have seen the power and results of others who achieved clarity of life purpose. Through the works of well-known and influential leaders, such as Reverend Dr. Martin Luther King Jr. and Nelson Mandela, and the achievements of ordinary people, the power that clarity of purpose holds in people's lives is evident. In this chapter, we provide a framework for you to begin, or for many of you to enhance, your journey toward increased consciousness and clarity about what you want to create in your life.

We have also seen the remarkable results that can be achieved by conscious and purposeful people working to forward the goals of an organization. As a transformational leader, a first step in creating a purposeful organization is to personally build a life of meaning. Consciousness at the scale of individual, group, or organization is at the heart of leading transformational change. Having an awareness of one's environment and one's own existence, emotions, sensations, and thoughts is a prerequisite to becoming a transformational leader within any organization. Clarity of life purpose, values, and direction in life are imperative to deliberate and productive growth. The most effective transformational leaders within organizations develop self-mastery and are clear about the connection of their personal vision with the vision of the organization.

It is the role of leaders within organizations to get to know their people and their interests and passions, what they truly care about. Organizations led by leaders who are highly skilled at leveraging the inherent, natural energy and interests of their employees hold a competitive edge in today's market. In fact, current research shows that the best way to retain talented individuals is to know them better than they know themselves and to customize their careers to those interests whenever possible.[1]

Consciousness of self opens the door to awareness or consciousness within a group. As individuals join together for a purpose, consciousness allows them to collectively monitor and openly discuss the group behavior, attitudes, aspirations, opinions, motives, or judgments that contribute to or hinder the group's progress.

Conscious individuals forming conscious groups working toward a shared purpose and vision are vital ingredients to creating a conscious enterprise. Consciousness of enterprise is seen when the entire organization has the ability to reflect and learn.

FRAMEWORK FOR CREATING
A LIFE OF MEANING

The integrated framework in Figure 8.1 is a powerful guide for designing a life of meaning and for coaching others in your organization in the area of self-mastery. This framework is not the only framework available for life planning, but it is a framework that we have used for over 20 years, and we know that it produces the desired results. In addition, the framework is accompanied by life planning tools, including the *life plan* and *conceptual image document*. These tools can be found in appendix A.

This framework and its related tools are designed to support emergence of your personal and spiritual energy.

VALUES

Your personal values are the deepest beliefs that direct your behavior. Values are the essential and enduring tenets by which one conducts life. Values serve as mental maps of the way you think things should be. They are your deepest convictions, and they are the primary filters through which you

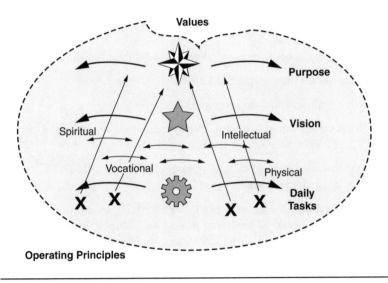

Figure 8.1 Leading a life of meaning.

view reality. Core values fundamentally shape one's life purpose, vision and actions taken throughout life.

In some situations, values are handed down from family or friends. People adopt these values unconsciously at a young age, and they often shape their lives unknowingly. At times, the values assumed from parents, left unexamined, can result in internal conflict when a belief or values system and a person's true purpose in life collide. Values are sourced from a deep and evolving understanding of purpose, often in an iterative process.

For these reasons, people who are pursuing self-mastery get clear about their personal values through introspection. Generally, a person should identify no more than five values during the life-planning process. Keeping the list of values to five or fewer helps to ensure that you are keenly aware of those values you hold most dear. If you list more than five values, you might not be capturing those that are most important to you. Your personal values in the truest sense are basic, fundamental, enduring, absolute, and irrevocable. In other words, even in a world of no agreement, you would not be persuaded to abandon your core values.

Community, freedom, love, equality, family, acceptance, contribution, and service are examples of values. In most cases, core values can be boiled down to a piercing simplicity that provides substantial guidance. Generally, core values are a single word. They are simple, straightforward and powerful. Values are powerful motivators, and they can help guide many decisions in life.

In thinking about your core values, consider the following questions:

What am I willing to get fired over?

What am I unwilling to give up, no matter what?

What values would I strive to live by even if the world ceased to reward me for having these values?

Which values would I be willing to discard if the world no longer favored them?

Organizations of Meaning spend time clarifying their ultimate values, the values they would be unwilling to give up, values they would die for. They understand that organizational values are more than just a few nice words displayed on a wall. The people within organizations of meaning live their values every day. Integrity between who we say we are, how we relate, and our actions is realized.

OPERATING PRINCIPLES

In life, as in organizations, core values are made operational with a set of operating principles, or ground rules. These principles can serve as guideposts for daily tasks and decision making. Operating principles often guide how people relate to others in life and in organizations. As a part of the life-planning process, write an operating principle for each value you hold. For an example, see Figure 8.2.

Value	Operating Principle
Acceptance	Open my heart to humanity
Service	Demonstrate love and caring in all that I do
Community	Support others, gather with others
Growth and development	Live in awe and wonder of the world
Truth	Be honest in my relationships, tell the truth

Figure 8.2 Operating principles.

LIFE PURPOSE

At the heart of your work in creating a life of meaning is gaining clarity of life purpose. Asking "What is my life's purpose?" can be humbling and calls upon courage for answers that are not always rapidly forthcoming. The investment in the search will begin to yield partial answers. Refinements over time will begin to paint a clearer picture, resulting in an understanding of your life purpose that becomes actionable, from which all the varying aspects of your life can flow from and towards. The dividends from this search for your life's purpose are enormous. The connection of life's pieces becomes evident, and synergies between different aspects of life spring forward.

Some people get so frustrated that the answer to this question does not fall from the sky and instantaneously transform their lives from boredom to joy. They give up even asking the question. Or worse yet, they may be resigned to living life without purpose. It doesn't matter anyway, right? Some of you are asking yourselves the question for the first time. Perhaps you are at a crossroads in your current career, seeking a new adventure, or have suffered a recent loss that has caused you to reevaluate your life. Wherever you are on the path, this framework and tools will assist you in moving ahead.

BE, DO, HAVE

According to the philosopher Jean Paul Sartre, all existence can be categorized under being, doing, or having. As an individual goes through life, he comes from *being,* a state of creativity, through doingness to havingness.[2] On the path to creating a life of meaning, you must first get in touch with these three basic aspects of life. *Being* is aliveness and consciousness. *Doing* is action and directed energy. *Having* is coming into possession of or acquiring. Each aspect of life supports the other two.[3]

A key to self-awareness is *to be* true to who you are, and then *to do* what gives you joy in order *to have* what you want. Unfortunately, many people approach this backwards. They seek first *to have* something in order *to do* something in order *to be* somebody. All you have to do is recall a recent cocktail party you attended to see the supremacy of this cultural mind-set at work in our lives. How many of the guests either shared their credentials or their job title as a way of introducing themselves? How many times were you asked, "What do you *do* for a living?" In contrast, when was the last time you were asked at a cocktail party "what do you really care about?" or "what do you have passion for?" or "what is your fundamental reason for being?" These questions would certainly alter the quality of your next party.

Let's look at another example. Take the process of becoming a physician. One might approach getting (*having*) a medical degree as the way to practice (*do*) medicine and thus become (*be*) a physician. On the other hand, as a healer (*be*) one might be involved (*do*) in the medical arts field and want to develop skills and benefit from the knowledge of others and, therefore, attend medical school. An outcome of attending medical school would be to *have* a medical degree.

People need to reorganize our customary mind-set of *have–do–be* to *be–do–have*. Failure to do so is a prescription for unhappiness as is so well articulated in Bartley's book *The Transformation of Man: Werner Erhard.* Erhard states:

> Untransformed life, life in the Mind state, is lived backward: life in the Mind state is an attempt to go from having, to doing to being—and to define one's identity in terms of what one has or does. As a result, one becomes imprisoned in havingness, which shapes doingness, and prevents one from achieving any longer the creativity of being. One becomes limited by what one possesses, including, especially, patterns of behavior, points of view, and systems of self-identification and preservation. One is indeed possessed by things. Life becomes circumscribed by self-created but seemingly intractable problems. One is the victim of circumstances: the past, the environment, relationships, and behavioral patterns. One is under the influence of everything one has gone through, done or achieved. To live this way is to live backward. Rather than achieving satisfaction from life, one becomes the slave to life. Love, health and happiness, and full self-expression are forfeit. The Mind state, by its nature, works to perpetuate rather than to solve problems.[4]

Gaining a clear life purpose from the *being* aspect of life can be achieved when you transcend what you think you must *have* or *do* in life and focus on what you truly care about. In other words, what brings you joy in life? After you have become clear about your overarching life purpose, you can begin to think about the question "what career or organization could I design that would allow me to more fully realize my life purpose?"

UNDERSTANDING YOUR LIFE PURPOSE

Understanding your life's purpose allows you to create, instead of simply reacting to your current environment. Without a life purpose, wandering aimlessly becomes the norm and it is often the source of boredom and frustration. Once your purpose is clarified, then you can begin to form your vision and goals to fulfill that purpose. With a directed vision and goals, your life's energy moves toward fulfilling that purpose and, thereby, grants meaning and joy to your everyday life.

Victor Frankl's book *Man's Search for Meaning* was groundbreaking not only because of the profound impact of his personal story of confinement to a Nazi concentration camp but also what he learned from this experience:

> Ultimately, man should not ask what the meaning of life is, but rather he must recognize that it is he who has asked . . . each man is questioned by life; and he can answer to life by answering for his own life; to life he can only respond by being responsible.[5]

Understanding life purpose requires introspection and commitment. It also requires you to look at what you are willing to be responsible for. This is perhaps the greatest challenge to discovering your life's purpose.

The *conceptual image document* is designed to help you clarify what you really care about. It poses the question: What brings you joy? What are your strengths and weaknesses? What do you have a passion for? All of these questions hold insights for you to your life's purpose.

Another avenue for clarifying your life's purpose is to interview the people who really know you. Ask your family and friends what is unique about you. Not just what you do, but how you go about doing it. Ask them to share with you situations where they perceived you were most alive. What were those situations? What about those situations was exciting to you? In the workplace or in life, when has time stood still for you and what was happening then? Can you recall a time when you were you most enlivened? What does it mean for you to have a rich, full life? All these questions hold valuable insights into your life purpose.

QUALITIES OF A POWERFUL LIFE PURPOSE

How you state your life purpose is important. Generally, the most powerful statement of life purpose is captured in a single phrase. For example, a life purpose might be ending world hunger, ensuring that *all* children are given the opportunity to learn, promoting creativity and full self-expression in the workplace, or celebrating what's right with the world.

All of these expressions of life purpose are reduced to a simple stated purpose. However, when you first begin the inquiry, the first expression of life purpose is rarely simple and powerfully stated. It can take years of self-reflection and refinement of life purpose to achieve that simple clarity. In the words of justice Oliver Wendell Holmes, "I wouldn't give a fig for the simplicity this side of complexity but I would give my life for the simplicity on the other side of complexity." You may find that the first version or even the tenth version of your life purpose is wordy and complicated. But over time, as you grow and live purposefully, you will refine and simplify your life purpose to a point where it reads like a slogan for whom you want to be in life. When it gets this simple and clear, your life purpose is ever present, directing your everyday actions and resulting in a purposeful, powerful, synergistic life.

PITFALLS IN UNDERSTANDING YOUR LIFE PURPOSE

Getting to an understanding of your reason for being, your life purpose, can be filled with impediments. Sticking points in the process of bringing consciousness to a life purpose sometimes causes abandonment of the search. But if you are prepared for some of the more common obstructions, it is hoped that you will simply move beyond these.

Framing Life Purpose As *Getting the Ideal Job*

Perhaps the biggest barrier to discovering life's purpose is a mind-set that often focuses on finding the really great job instead of looking at a broader purpose for life. We often hear people complain that "if I only had *that* promotion with *that* salary, then I'd really be happy." Overfocusing on finding that ideal job, discovering what career you want to pursue, or going after that next promotion as a way of achieving happiness misses the point of creating a life of meaning. It causes suffering and loss of energy when you're without the *ideal job*. And when you get the ideal job, the joy you gain is often short-lived. Life purpose is bigger than the position that you hold. It is a commitment to fulfill something beyond a job description or title. It transcends position so that life purpose can be fulfilled in any position you hold or don't hold.

Limiting Life Purpose to Self-Interest

Some people get caught in the trap that life purpose is solely personal—about what I need to achieve or to have in life. In many ways, life purpose can, and should, be about your self-interest. For example, a person's life purpose could be stated as *being successful*. This overarching purpose is broad and offers an individual the opportunity to take actions for achieving goals at work and in life. This life purpose is also not inherently dependent on holding a specific job function or title (unless that is how you define success). In truth, you have the potential to fulfill this life purpose in any position that offers you a chance to create success. These are certainly some of the strengths of this life purpose. However, framing your life purpose solely in this way can have its limitations. Rather than inspiring you to act, it can wear you down by having to achieve goal after goal. In many ways, being successful is the unconscious life purpose that many people have been living and has driven them to the point of exhaustion and disappointment.

In our experience of coaching hundreds of people in clarifying their life purpose, identifying a purpose that both includes and transcends self-interest holds the most power for people. In the words of Reverend Dr. Martin Luther King Jr.:

> Every man must decide if he will walk in the light of creative altruism or the darkness of destructive selfishness. This is the judgment. Life's most persistent and urgent question is, what are you doing for others?

Failure to Understand that Life Purpose Is Both Discovered and Declared

The inquiry about life purpose is indeed a discovery *process*. Unfortunately, people relate to the process like there is something (a life purpose) outside of us that they need to find. Robert Fritz, in his book *Creating,* explains:

> The notion that you can discover what matters presumes that what matters somehow already exists, and that it is the thing itself that is generative. Rather than bringing your energy, talents and interests to what you want, you search for the "right" thing to "turn you on." If the original generative force does not come from you but from the thing itself, you will eventually run out of energy, interest and involvement. Your expectations will lead to disappointments, and you will search for something else.[6]

The process of *discovery* which can be achieved through inquiry into your life's purpose is important. However, this is only half the equation. In fact, gaining clarity of life purpose necessitates that you actually *declare* your purpose in life somewhere during the discovery process. A key barrier to achieving this clarity is getting trapped in the inquiry, waiting for some external force to let you know that you have identified the perfect life purpose.

Thinking There Is Only One "Perfect" Life Purpose for You

Many people get hung up on discovering the *one perfect* life purpose. They allow this preoccupation with finding that one unique reason for being to stop them from declaring any life purpose at all. People get trapped in the inquiry and never take a stand for what they're about in life. The moment they get excited about the progress made in discerning a life purpose, they quickly question whether that's really it. Understanding that your life purpose is a continuous process of refinement and incisive inquiry, rather than finding that one perfect purpose, can promote freedom to play in the inquiry. Declare a life purpose that feels right in the moment, knowing that you have the freedom to refine your life purpose over time.

VISION

Vision's connection to purpose is critical in producing an *on-purpose* life and leading a life of meaning. With clarity of life's purpose, one can create a powerful and purposeful vision for life. We recommend that you develop a five-year vision that encompasses all aspects of your life. Without an arrival point and a defined future state, your life journey becomes little more than a random walk through life. There is nothing fundamentally wrong with this approach to living. We have simply found that it is insufficient when your desire is to produce specific and purposeful results in life.

Creating your five-year vision will require that you take risks and be honest with yourself, sometimes painfully so. What do you truly desire to create in the next five years? It takes courage and commitment to declare a future.

Your five-year vision should inspire you, and it should encompass all aspects of your life. It should paint a vivid picture of what you desire your life to be in five years. The vision is not formed from a position of hope but of declaration. In other words, you are declaring your intention to create that life. In addition, by bringing that vision into existence you are naturally fulfilling your life's purpose. We recommend that you create your five-year vision by imaging that you are standing in that future state. Write your vision down as having already been accomplished.

The life-planning process also promotes the creation of mini visions for different aspects of your life such as intellectual, vocational, health, family, and spirit. The life-planning framework provided in appendix A is highly flexible, so you should freely customize the domains and areas of your life and name them as you see fit. We strongly encourage you to create life domains and areas that represent all aspects of life, so that you can represent your life as a whole person. A mini vision for each area of your life, a *point of arrival* is typically a 12-month vision. Each year, you would update the mini visions for your life with the intention of closing the gap between the current year's life plan and your five-year vision.

Visions are launched and accomplished in a lifelong journey. In other words, vision creation is an ongoing process. Once you begin the journey of life planning, you will find the value and power it holds in your ability to produce purposeful results and to achieve your desired futures.

DAILY TASKS

In life, people are often confronted by the very real experience that they simply never have enough time to complete all their daily tasks. They begin to set in opposition one part of life against another. More simply put, many people see themselves juggling competing commitments with limited success. This way of viewing life is one of *separation* of the different aspects of life and trying to achieve balance between all parts. For example, the current view of work *versus* family as a problem to be solved is a key issue for many people. We believe it is the mind-set itself, *aspects of life are separate,* which actually originates the issue. A solution is to consider the whole first and foremost in all endeavors and not simply refine the pieces to make a more productive whole. This requires a shift in the current mind-set from which leaders view their own lives and the lives of their employees.

It is a challenging shift. Ken Wilber, in his book *A Brief History of Everything*, speaks from this position when he refers to transcending the problems of today with broader perspectives and creations of tomorrow. A broader perspective needed in the balance of work *versus* family is that they both flow from the same source, a personal life purpose. And when that individually tailored life purpose is brought to consciousness, the balance equation no longer applies. Life pieces and daily tasks flow from this purpose and exist in harmony, not in conflict and competition for time. In this example, work begins to flow from, towards, and throughout lives as people easily imagine their family doing.

HAVING CONVERSATIONS ABOUT LIFE PURPOSE IN YOUR ORGANIZATION

Achieving transformation of any organization requires people within the organization to understand where they are going in life and how life's energy connects to their work. So how do you address the search for individual's life purpose across an organization? Well, a different conversation is needed from leadership. First, a leader openly shares his or her life's purpose and how that purpose determines the organizational direction being pursued by the leader. Then, instead of leadership filling in the blanks for their employees in terms of what their life's purpose should be, the transformational leader takes on the role of coach, helping others discover their unique purpose. Alignment of these life energies is then accomplished. Methodologies are currently being used in large organizations that follow this simple but involved course of collective consciousness toward a shared vision. The difference is letting whole individuals, with all their life pieces, show up at work and discover that their energy is directed toward a joint vision—not concentrated on manipulation to derive short-term compliance.

So how are innovative companies using this different mind-set? They start with the hiring process. "Why are you here?" becomes a key question. "What have you done" and "what qualifications do you have?" become only supporting information. In addition, strategic planning is now being checked against energy for accomplishment, not just whether or not the plan is the right one. This is because, when investigating failed strategies in the business sector, the reason for failure most often cited was not that the strategy was wrong, it was simply that the strategy was not accomplished. Finding out if there is any energy or commitment to accomplishing a strategy (flowing from and toward the collective purpose) can save a lot of wasted energy and expectations.

Furthermore, work plans become part of a more holistic life plan. The work plan integrates an individual's life plan as part of the business setting. Declarations about life purpose, joy-giving experiences, and creative intentions are shared in a very natural way throughout the organization.

SUMMARY LEARNINGS

1. Leading others requires that you be awake and conscious of your own life direction.

2. Clarity of life purpose, vision, values, and goals are fundamental in creating a life of meaning.

3. Putting action toward your plan produces results.

TO ACTION

1. What is your comprehensive life plan? Formulate one.

2. How can you share your life plan with other people within and outside of work?

3. Can you reflect on and integrate relevant feedback?

4. What is the best way to maintain a current life plan over time?

ENDNOTES

1. Timothy Butler and James Waldroop, "The Art of Retaining Your Best People," *Harvard Business Review on Point in Pursuit of Productivity: The Business Case For Passion* (Boston, MA: Harvard Business School Publishing, Product Number 4282, 2002): 22.
2. W. W. Bartley III, *The Transformation of a Man: Werner Erhard*, (New York: Clarkson N. Potter Publishers, 1978): 207.
3. Stephen Hacker, Marta Wilson, and Cindy Johnston, *Work Miracles* (Blacksburg, VA: Insight Press, 1999): 44.
4. See note 2.
5. Victor Frankl, *Man's Search for Meaning* (New York: Washington Square Press, 1959): 131.
6. Robert Fritz, *Creating* (New York: Ballentine Books, 1991): 181.

LEADERSHIP VIGNETTE

Jeanette Fish

Leadership Position: Assistant manager of employment service programs

Organization: Oregon Employment Department

Transformational Results: Developed a highly successful, one-stop service delivery model at the Job and Career Center in Salem, Oregon. Jeanette Fish led her staff and the broader community partners to design and implement a newly integrated service delivery program that better serves jobseekers and Oregon employers. This effort required the employment department staff to collaborate in new ways with the broader group of community partners to plan for the change, to align around a common vision, and to set achievable goals. Today, this center is seen as a highly customer-focused and user-friendly career center, an excellent benchmark for other organizations. In recognition of their efforts in creating a one-stop service delivery model, the local workforce investment board formally certified the Job and Career Center.

Reflections on Transformation[1]

What contributed to the success of this change initiative?

The commitment of the staff and community partners to provide the highest quality of service was a key factor in our success. We were willing to change, to take risks, and to do things differently, so that we could better serve our customers. We were all willing to listen to one another. Frequent communication occurred, including a weekly meeting and daily five-minute stand-up meetings to ensure a human connection. We made sure to bring humor to our work, and we took special care to be supportive of someone who had a rough day. Personally, I never asked anyone to do something I wasn't willing to do myself. I was very honest with people. We talked about the struggles, acknowledged difficulties, and allowed people to vent so long as they did so with a commitment to move forward. It was important for me to provide encouragement on many levels and to take accountability for my decisions.

What are your reflections on the role of a life plan in your own growth and ability to lead others?

A definite turning point for me in my leadership style was to bring my passion and caring for other people to the work setting. In understanding my life plan, I realized the importance of caring for people and I wanted to express that more at work by building relationships. I started to spend extra time with people. I began to ask them about their family and their interests and to simply talk with them after a difficult interaction with a jobseeker. Prior to this, I had it in my mind that I had to be solely focused on being productive, my image of what I thought a leader should be. Also, in my journey from manager to leader, I moved from a technical expert to a nonexpert. I had to totally rely on the staff, yet I felt I should know it all. Not being a subject-matter expert forced me to think differently by focusing on bringing out the good ideas in others and, in doing so, it helped me to shift from manager to leader. Over time, I overcame needing to know the answer and began more and more to draw upon the strengths of the team.

What are your learnings in your coaching of others?

As a coach, it is important to be an attentive listener. Over time, I have quieted myself and learned to listen more. I have also moved away from trying to figure things out for people. Through listening, a person can come to his or her own understanding about how to best solve the problem. I am much slower to give advice.

What contributed to your success in moving from management to leadership?

I have had great mentors, people who supported me and provided me with a lot of feedback. These mentors were not all at higher levels; some were people who worked for me and were willing to be very honest when I asked for feedback. Really, I think as I move along, I see myself as a servant. My role as a leader is to provide the environment, atmosphere, and tools that people need to be successful. I am already starting to see these leadership ideas grow and flourish in others. Perhaps the people that work for me now will be leading me someday.

ENDNOTE

1. Transcript excerpts, interview with Jeanette Fish, March 7, 2003, Salem, Oregon, conducted by Tammy Roberts.

9

Mind-Sets for Performance

In this chapter, we reflect on the new competitive requirement of awakened spirits in the workplace and the role of life purpose in authentic expression of spirit. We then explore how individual and collective mind-sets can retard or accelerate that expression of spirit and, ultimately, hinder or promote transformation within the organization. Distinguishing mind-sets is the mental agility to see the mental maps that inform your thoughts and actions. It is the reflection and discovery of the background conversation or larger context that informs spoken words. Mind-sets appear as points of view about self, others, and your view of what is possible within your organization or unit. Mind-sets are ever present; they serve as your vista of the world.

Understanding mind-sets and their role in performance is critical as a transformational leader. The mental maps from which you and your organization operate fundamentally bind the world of opportunity available to your organization and ultimately to your success in producing breakthrough performance. Ben Zander and Rosamund Stone Zander explain:

> We perceive only the sensations we are programmed to receive, and our awareness is further restricted by the fact that we recognize only those for which we have mental maps or categories.[1]

Left undistinguished, mind-sets can significantly hinder or block performance. For example, a victim mind-set can consume the energy of an organization and kill off spirit. The tendency of the victim mind-set is to give up, blame others, or only work harder when faced with barriers. Instead, a fundamental shift from this nonproductive mind-set to an at-cause mind-set is needed to catalyze desired transformation.

AWAKENING SPIRITS

At one time, *steady* and *compliant* were considered model traits for a person desiring to move ahead within an organization. Following the explicit instructions of the boss produced support from above and the subsequent benefits. And such contracts still exist in a shrinking number of workplaces. Still, many organizations simply require the absence of problem creators, where staying under the radar is sufficient. Such an approach to work could be accomplished by a spirited person for a short period of time. But after a while, the spirit either moves on or becomes subdued. Suppression of spirit has been, and is presently, the state of many organizations, whether conscious or unconscious in its execution.

When the choice is made to subordinate spirit in an organization, it is like having the workforce fall asleep. And don't be confused: sleeping on the job can be done without eyes being shut. Yes, direct confrontation is a benefit derived from having a docile workforce, but as John Stuart Mill writes in his essay *On Liberty*, "A state which dwarfs its people, so that they may be more docile instruments in its hand, even for the most beneficial reasons, will find that with small men no great things can be accomplished." Likewise, an organization which dwarfs its people will find little energy or creativity in its workforce, and as a result have low performance in the market.

Oh, you can rouse up the troops for short duration with individual threats of job action or impending economic disaster for the organization as a whole. But this usually turns sleep to victimhood followed by resentment. So, to avoid such results and move to capturing the creativity needed for transforming an organization, awakening the spirits of all persons in the workplace is a critical starting point.

From the individual perspective, discovering a life purpose brings forth the spirit. Individuals having consumed the basics of life (many to gluttonous proportions) are discovering that hygienic needs have been satisfied many times over. The search is on for *what life is really all about.* And with this search under way, people are waking up from a television-induced, societal numbing existence. These personal renaissances can be initiated with major life challenges, personal crises, age, job loss, or from just noticing the quickening passage of time with age. When life's purpose becomes a subject for investigation, renewed vigor is a noticeable outcome, often accompanied by new adventures in reading, exercise, and varied interests. Likewise, denying a call to live a purposeful life can have devastating impacts on health, spirit, and relationships. It is not easy to start achieving higher performance without a crystal clear purpose, but in starting, you find clarity.

ROLE MODELS

We often use famous persons, historical and living, to illustrate that maintaining a strong drive to conduct a fulfilling life yields spectacular results when combined with transformational leadership. Mother Theresa, Reverend Dr. Martin Luther King Jr., Nelson Mandela, Gandhi, Joe Lewis, and Michel Jordan are the names often pulled from our common references.

However, the same evidence of leadership and personal drive exists in others of unsavory value sets like Adolf Hitler, Jim Jones, Idi Amin, and Saddam Hussein. We don't need to invoke the value overlay prior to examining the effectiveness of the personal drive. Certainly values must be considered, but not necessarily in evaluating effectiveness. Match the transformational effect of a person's drive on each person's system of selected influence.

Famous people can teach us something, even if the myth takes over from reality. However, what can be even more engaging is to see where focus on a life purpose has garnered spectacular results in our own lives.

THE POWER OF MIND-SETS IN PERFORMANCE

Mind-sets are the distinctive viewpoints that determine how people see the world. Mind-sets are formulated from life experiences, the summary meaning people gave to life from childhood to adult life. In self, mind-sets dictate what people perceive to be possible; they define mental boundaries and ultimately the actions people take. They inform the quality of relationships with others and define what is possible for an organization. The power of thought is awesome. Thoughts create our reality. Take the example of Mark, for instance.

As a child, Mark grew up in a low-income family where he was one of six children. Most evenings, Mark went to bed hungry as there was simply not enough food to go around. In high school, Mark never went to ball games or movies because his family could not afford it. Throughout his life, the mantra was "you can't go or you can't have that because we don't have the money." College was not a possibility either, so he took a job at the local grocery store. He later married, had two children, and eventually was promoted to management in the grocery store. The family continued to just make ends meet, closely tracking expenses and adhering to a strict budget.

As a manager at the store, Mark was perceived as a person who was effective in running the store and keeping within budget, but his employees frequently complained that he was a micromanager. The financial health of the store was stable but nothing to brag about. Mark worked very hard but never felt he did enough. He lived in an incessant state of worry that he would fail.

Mark's view of life, formulated as a child, is one of a scarcity mentality. His adoption of a scarcity mind-set was an unconscious choice. He lives in a world where the pie is never big enough to go around. When the scarcity mind-set is left unconscious, or seen as an experience that happens to him rather than a choice, Mark fails to see the abundance that life has to offer.

In their important book *The Art of Possibility,* the Zanders agree that one's state of mind determines what one sees as possible:

> Our premise is that many of the circumstances that seem to block us in our daily lives may only appear to do so based on a framework of assumptions we carry with us. Draw a different frame around the same set of circumstances and new pathways come into view. Find the right framework and extraordinary accomplishment becomes everyday experience.[2]

By bringing consciousness to the scarcity mind-set, Mark has the opportunity to shift that mind-set to one of abundance and to draw a different frame of life. In doing so, a world of possibility would open to Mark. Holding a mind-set of abundance, Mark would physically and intellectually enlarge his vista. He would have more opportunities and choices available to him simply by changing his mind-set. Easier said than done perhaps, but it is possible.

MIND-SETS AT WORK

A primary role of the transformational leader is to know the spirits present within the organization and to align and attune those spirits toward the organization's vision. In an effective organization of meaning, members of the top leadership team develop a deeper connection with the *uniqueness* of each individual within and outside their unit. Transformational leaders seek to understand the passion and interests of each person and suspend personal agendas. The goals are to first and foremost understand what the other person is really about and then look for the individual's vector of energy for the organization.

Engaging another in a conversation about life purpose and personal vision is a powerful approach to uncovering the unique energy or life force held within. Life planning is an excellent tool for individuals to clarify what is important in life and how their work fits in with the larger direction of their life. The first step to leading transformational change is to create your own life plan. With this in hand, you can be authentic in supporting others to create a life of meaning.

Setting your course in life is the necessary first step. However, even with clarity of direction and deeper understanding of your life purpose, this is often insufficient to produce breakthrough change in lives, relationships, and organizations. Bringing moment-to-moment consciousness to your own mental models is imperative.

Mind-sets are at play in the individual, in relationships, and in the organization as a whole. Unproductive mind-sets can derail any great plan. Having a life plan is the starting point of leading a life of meaning (and ultimately an organization of meaning). However, mind-sets—how you see the world—are ever present, acting as filters to hinder or accelerate your direction in life and movement toward goals. This is because mind-sets serve as the thinking behind people's experience of the world.

Thinking determines people's actions in life. What people think becomes their reality. For example, if your mind-set is focused on scarcity, you are most likely to take limited actions in life, shying away from the boldness in action that is possible in life. If your mind-set is one of projecting (or protecting) your image, this mind-set can dictate every action in your life. Life becomes about sustaining an image, which often has little to do with who a person truly is. Typically, image making is about projecting material wealth, an advanced degree, position in an hierarchy, intellectual quickness, and the list goes on. Image making is energy-draining. The opportunity is to bring an authentic mind-set within self and in relationship with others. It is about living in integrity with your spirit, what you truly care about. Authenticity allows for the possibility of not having to know it all and living in the possibility of tapping the collective knowledge and wisdom to move your organization forward.

All actions produce some result in life whether to advance a goal or to sabotage or go against desired results. This book is about producing breakthrough results or discontinuous change in results. As a leader, seeing how your own mind-sets hinder or advance your results is important. Feedback is an excellent source of information to discern your own mental models (see Figure 9.1).

Feedback on results comes in a variety of forms. It comes from family, friends, and colleagues in the form of disappointment, celebration, joy, anger, evaluation, or coaching, to name a few. It also comes from within with self-appraisal or judgment. The physical body provides people with feedback, although largely ignored, in the form of pain, stress, anxiety, exuberance, or vitality. People live in a world of *neck-ups* and would benefit

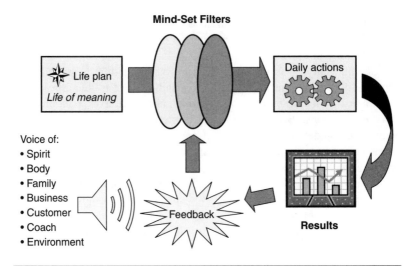

Figure 9.1   Mind-set filtering our life plans.

from more conscious connection to the feedback the body provides. In the business setting, you receive feedback from customers, suppliers, vendors, and other individuals, groups, or organizations throughout the entire value exchange.

Both positive and negative feedback provides an opportunity to build consciousness of the mind-sets at play in self. For example, Susan declared in her life plan the desire to lose 25 pounds in 2003. Six months into the year, her body had not changed. In addition, her trainer complained that she frequently misses her scheduled sessions. Susan declared one result and produced a different result. Does this sound familiar? The opportunity is for Susan to engage in a deeper exploration of her mind-set around losing weight. In doing so, Susan discovers the thinking that is informing her actions, or in this case, the lack thereof. Her mind-set goes like this: Everyone in her family is overweight, and it is so hard for her to lose those last few pounds. In addition, Susan travels extensively for her job, so she simply does not have access to the proper exercise equipment nor the time to work out. To top it off, she frequently has to quickly grab lunch at the nearest fast food restaurant between client meetings. In other words, rather than holding an intentional mind-set to reach her target weight goal, she succumbs to the mechanisms of life. Left undistinguished, Susan is condemned to the annual cycle of committing to lose weight and failing to do so. Once distinguished, she can consciously make the choice of a causal approach to weight loss, or she can simply give in to the victim mind-set in this area of her life.

In your organization, people hold different points of view or mind-sets. These mind-sets play out at the individual, group, and organizational levels. In a sense, the organization itself is the product of the collective mind that views it. As such, it is critical as transformational leader that you understand your own mind-sets and enhance your ability to see mind-sets at play in others. Finally, expanding your capacity to coach others to generate a fundamental shift in mind-set is a chief leverage area in producing transformation.

MIND-SET CHOICES

Adopting a mind-set is actually a choice. It just seems like mind-sets *happen to us* with little or no choice because people are asleep to their own thinking process. Unproductive mind-sets become most apparent in the face of a breakdown or crisis, when emotions are high and people become even more unconscious. Unfortunately, even in this situation, the mind-set is often only apparent to others, and you fail to see it. Mind-sets are often blind spots.

When done consciously, mind-set choices produce different outcomes. Peter McWilliams expressed this in his book *You Can't Afford the Luxury of a Negative Thought*:

> Positive thoughts (joy, happiness, fulfillment, achievement, worthiness) have positive results (enthusiasm, calm, well-being, ease, energy, love). Negative thoughts (judgment, unworthiness, mistrust, resentment, fear) produce negative results (tension, anxiety, alienation, anger, fatigue).[3]

But he is far from the first person to see the power of mind-set choices. Major religions speak to the wisdom of choosing productive, life-giving mental choices. And for the transformational leader, these mind-set choices put into motion resources way beyond the individual. The mind-set choices are both infectious and cultural foundation pillars.

It takes a high degree of commitment to begin the journey of understanding yourself at a deeper level. It takes courage to look at and accept, without self-judgment, the self-imposed barriers you fashion. But the rewards of self-knowledge are great. In doing so, you can shift your mind-set from one that holds your life hostage to a mind-set for performance. The Dalai Lama states:

If we wish to lessen the power of negative emotions, we must search for the causes that give rise to them. We must work at removing or uprooting those causes.[4]

In our years of working with people, groups, and organizations, we have identified a set of polarity mind-sets that are fundamental to what it is to be a human being and also what is possible in being human. You will recognize many of these mind-sets. The purpose of the modeling is to give you the ability to more clearly see what mind-sets are operational in you and in others. We first present the five mind-sets that retard performance. These five are fundamental to what it is to be a human being because they are directly related to our instinctual drive for survival. They were formulated at a very young age as our mind cataloged perceived threats to our continued existence. Through his study of the working of the mind, Werner Erhard has this to say:

> The mind is a device whose purpose or, more accurately, design function is to ensure the survival of oneself or of anything that one identifies with oneself. Survival, in the sense intended, goes beyond physical survival. It includes the survival of one's ideas, opinions and self-conceptions, and thus results in being right and making others wrong, dominating and avoiding domination, justifying oneself and invalidating others. To accomplish its purpose, the Mind scrupulously records those experiences that are necessary for survival. Among the latter are those records containing pain and unconsciousness; loss or shock associated with emotional stress; and unwitting reminders of earlier records containing pain, shock or loss. Whenever the present environment resembles in any way some such painful or stressful memory, whenever one encounters a situation that one perceives as threatening to survival—one in which one might lose, be made wrong, be dominated, be invalidated—the past memories are reactivated, called into play in an undiscriminating way, as guides to the avoidance of pain and threat.[5]

Survival is a human condition. This condition sets the mind (you) on a course to formulate five unproductive mind-sets, while at the same time falsifying their ultimate, long-term value (see Figure 9.2).

In our work with people within organizations, and through our study of the body of knowledge in mind-set management, we have identified five unproductive mind-sets that are at play within individuals and groups. A brief description of the characteristics of each mind-set follows.

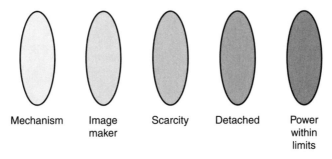

Figure 9.2 Five mind-sets retarding performance.

Mechanism

- Victim state of being

- Barriers determine success

- Excuses made to match degree of failure

- Live at the effect of nature and occurrences

Image maker

- Appearance paramount

- Belief in the ability to hide inner self

- Dishonest

- Out of integrity

Scarcity

- Restricted possibilities

- More involved, less the opportunities

- Self-embracing

- Exclusive

Detachment

- Focus on division

- Little connection between life

- Independent variables

- Reliance on self

Power within limits

- Restricted power

- Hierarchically granted

- Positional power required to succeed

- Self-worth tied to position

The five unproductive mind-sets are easy to see, particularly in others. In a sense, they have an autopilot nature to them. We can turn them on in two seconds flat. The challenge is to recognize them for what they are— a point of view, a thought, a context. In this sense, they are invented by the mind and supported by the evidence people view in the world. Evidence seen only because people hold that mind-set in the first place. This becomes a vicious circle of mind-set producing evidence and evidence reinforcing mind-set. People set mind-set traps for themselves that hold them in a persistent place of nonperformance.

You have a choice. Given that mind-sets are invented, why not invent another way of seeing the world.

In contrast to these five unproductive mind-sets are five mind-sets that when adopted can result in breakthrough results (see Figure 9.3). The five mind-sets for performance are listed following, along with their characteristics.

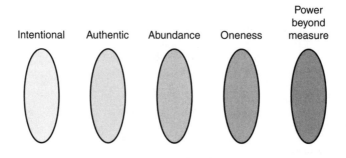

Figure 9.3 Five mind-sets for performance.

Intention

- Understanding the causal nature of being
- Conscious creation
- Leveraging barriers
- Discarding excuses

Authentic

- Truth of great importance
- Transparency
- Forthright and honest
- Living in integrity

Abundance

- Unrestricted possibilities
- The more involved, the more the opportunities
- Energy embracing
- Inclusive

Oneness

- Seeing ourselves in others
- Understanding life's connections
- Wisdom
- Indivisibility of existence

Power beyond measure

- Unrestricted influence
- Alignment of energies
- Emotional quotient
- Tapping into the greater

Adopting a productive mind-set is actually a generative process. In other words, it requires consciousness and commitment to live a life of purpose and possibility. The choice is between surviving or living with the possibility of being human: the possibility of intention, authenticity, abundance, oneness, and power beyond measure. The Zanders describe the new leader in the following way:

> The new leader carries the distinction that it is the framework of fear and scarcity, not scarcity itself, that promotes divisions between people. He asserts we can create the conditions for emergence of anything that is missing. We are living in the land of our dreams. This leader calls upon our passion rather than our fear. She is the relentless architect of the possibility that human beings can be.[6]

COACHING OTHERS IN MIND-SET DISCOVERY

Coaching is acknowledged as a newly required skill of leaders and managers at all levels of an organization. In recent years, numerous books have been published on the topic of coaching in the workplace and offering hundreds of techniques. However, to produce transformational or discontinuous change, something more than coaching techniques or tools is required. Coaching in the context of transformational leadership involves having the ability and the authentic desire to awaken spirit in another. It involves raising consciousness and clarity to personal purpose, vision, and values in others. According to Robert Hargrove:

> The key to becoming a masterful coach lies in having a dream, aspiration, and the bone-deep commitment to make a difference in the lives of individuals, groups, or entire organizations. It is that commitment that is the alchemical chamber in which great coaches are born. It is that commitment that unlocks your wisdom, intuition, and insight when mere technique fails.[7]

Transformational coaching is not about having the right answer or offering counsel. The first step in transformational coaching is to relate to another on a spirit-to-spirit level. Conversations focused on personal passion, life vision, and purpose are the building blocks to this deeper connection. Taking sincere interest in the whole person is required. Manipulation to your agenda or showing false interest will simply not work.

Being able to articulate a set of performance mind-sets and their unproductive polarity is useful in bringing yourself and others to higher levels of consciousness. Developing your own ability to powerfully trade off an unproductive mind-set for a productive one equips you with the ability to coach others. Only then can you engage others in seeing their own mind-sets. Through the discovery of your own experience in mind-set management, you will better understand how to approach others. Without this self-discipline and mastery, top leaders typically fall into the trap of using mind-sets like a weapon against nonproductive employees.

Coaching is not about telling someone what is not working but rather asking another person to reflect on his or her own mind-set. Coaching is aiding others in their own self-discovery and reflection. It involves powerful questions, not answers, and a firm commitment to the greatness of others.

SUMMARY LEARNINGS

1. Living a life of meaning is unmatched in its effectiveness, regardless of value sets.

2. Understanding your calling and purpose is a continuous process of refinement and incisive inquiry.

3. Remain on-purpose and results come forth.

4. Mind-sets filter your performance as you move to fulfill life's purpose and move toward a vision.

5. The primary mind-sets for performance are abundance, power beyond measure, oneness, intention, and authenticity.

TO ACTION

1. Can you clearly state what you most care about in life?

2. Can you develop a short list of people you observe with a strong life's purpose and discover their process for developing and discovering their calling?

3. Can you each day, for the next 30 days, write down the mind-sets you see in yourself and in others? When a nonproductive mind-set is at play in you, make a conscious choice to shift to a productive mind-set.

ENDNOTES

1. Ben Zander and Rosamund Stone Zander, *The Art of Possibility* (Boston: Harvard Business School Press, 2000): 10.
2. Ibid, 1.
3. Peter McWilliams, *You Can't Afford the Luxury of a Negative Thought* (Los Angeles: Prelude Press, 1995): 11.
4. Dalai Lama, *An Open Heart: Practicing Compassion in Everyday Life,* Edited by Nicholas Vreeland (Boston: Little, Brown and Company, 2001): 61.
5. W. W. Bartley III, *The Transformation of Man, Werner Erhard* (New York: Clarkson N. Potter Publishers, 1978): 185.
6. Zander and Zander, 165.
7. Robert Hargrove, *Masterful Coaching* (San Francisco: Jossey-Bass/Pfeiffer, 2003): 13.

10

Taking Ideas to Action

Assuming you have stayed with this text until the tenth chapter due to perceived value of the transformational leadership approach, how to take action on these ideas is probably in your thoughts. How do you and your organization adopt the model and mind-sets addressed? What are the most efficient and effective ways of having leaders see both the necessity of transformational leadership and gain the skills to practice the art?

CULTIVATING INDIVIDUAL SKILLS

If it were as straightforward as "proceed through steps 1–12," the acquisition of transformational leadership skills would need little individual consciousness. It would be pleasant to just sign up for a two-day leadership course and walk out a renaissance leader equipped with the skills and a certificate in hand. But more is needed than a course. To internalize the truths in the transformational leadership model requires knowledge, practice, and a high level of individual and collective consciousness. The number of decisions and the complexity of actions presented within an organization's daily life require that the abstractions of transformational leadership be understood and that decisions incorporate the principles and lessons contained. Where to start? The following seven broad areas should be addressed in order to build leadership capacity as an individual.

Review Current Results

Given that transformational leadership is about creating positive, discontinuous results, it is important to know what results are currently being produced.

Analyze both corporate and individual leadership results. Where are results lacking? Where are results strong? Determine the performance outages.

Embrace Mind-Sets for Performance

Build mental agility in order to recognize the mind-sets at work inside of you. Using the five mind-sets for performance, check which mind-set resides inside and build the capacity to spend more time in productive mind-sets. Avoid lecturing others on how they can improve, but instead focus on your own mind-set. Set aside time for self-reflection. Review your actions not in a harsh, judgmental manner, but use more of an objective viewer stance in looking at how you operate.

Focus on the Possibility

What are the levels of performance that would constitute breakthrough? Play with challenges of huge proportion. What step-functional increase in performance would produce the most dramatic results impacting the entire organization? What area is a likely target? What is currently seen as a barrier that, if removed, huge gains could be accomplished? Bring daring targets into focus.

Adopt a Model

Build a model to capture your transformational leadership ideas. We have presented a model. Adjust and make alterations to it that best represent your thinking. Have a reference model where you can anchor your experiments with leadership.

Evaluate Skills

Understand your present skill set. Use the transformational leadership evaluation found in appendix B. What skills will propel you toward breakthrough performance? Where are your biggest opportunities? Concentrate on producing meaningful expansion of these skills.

Develop a Personalized Plan

What plan do you have for acquiring the skills needed? Beyond training, how do you plan to field test your new knowledge and take up a bold practice regiment? Like all good plans, detailed actions supported by expected performance criteria should be incorporated.

Lead Anew

After all the preparatory work, move into practicing the new leadership approach. Take risks and act boldly. Sometimes people believe time is inexhaustible and that taking slow measured steps will produce individual leadership growth over the long run. Another point of view is *this is it?* This is the last chance you have to produce stellar results through your leadership. For whatever reason, there will be no tomorrow to practice new skills. With such an outlook, the risk is in not taking bold action. So what are you waiting for? Why are you hesitating, not risking it all?

It is that easy—and that difficult. Review results, embrace productive mind-sets, and set high performance goals for yourself and your organization while building transformational skills in deficient areas. The key is to take concrete steps and risks toward cultivating a transformational leadership skill set utilizing a high level of consciousness to discern effectiveness along the way. Courage to challenge your leadership techniques will be essential. And understand, these present leadership techniques under reconstruction were the ones that drove your success to date. Thus, there is the need for courage to risk faltering at first.

ADVANCING COLLECTIVE LEADERSHIP

Seeing the opportunity to drive a different level of organizational performance by having leaders utilize a transformational leadership orientation speaks to awareness. Having leaders actually employ the approach speaks to leadership development. And when leadership development is attended to, the tendency is to move to corporate leadership training in a classroom setting. With such a move, role modeling transformational leadership goes right out the door. Transformational leadership is about jumping up performance. Training in such a manner has not shown dramatic change in leadership performance. Training by leadership methodologies alone is insufficient without application on the job. Leaders may be inspired by new ideas and approaches, but not until their application do the learnings take root. Only through practice and observation of actual results do leaders internalize the learnings. So, by all means, undertake training to introduce leadership ideas and new methods. But build-in application through demonstration projects and reflections. Have leaders lead with the new methods, have leaders commit to transformational results, and then discover the methods that best suit them.

Give enterprising leadership assignments to those undergoing the knowledge enhancement. What are the results areas screaming for breakthrough? Have leaders stepped forward in these areas and committed to produce such results? Augment with intellectual capacity from within and outside the organization. But have the leader move to put the learnings into practice. Use the learnings from these assignments to build confidence and make corrective actions to their leadership approach.

Susan Burnett, vice president of workforce development and organization effectiveness at Hewlett-Packard, commented on leadership development training:

> Executive development is not about creating a university or a lineup of great speakers. It is about bringing new knowledge, new practices, and new thinking to the challenges of the day. Bring in industry and academic experts in the context of the challenge and have them become thinking partners with your senior executives. Make sure the objectives are clear and the measures are real. You'll have executives beating the door down to sign up.[1]

Use the classroom and accomplished trainers to present transformational leadership learnings, but do it within the context of the current work challenges.

Coaching others in adopting mind-sets for performance is a chief leverage area for producing transformation. These mind-sets are like filters. With a life purpose and a plan, the filters you choose either enhance or retard your progress. As previously cautioned, you should be grappling with your own mind-sets at the outset, building capacity to adopt a different mind-set within yourself first.

Pull together a collective approach to transforming your organization's leadership. The following four elements compose the approach.

Share the Transformation Leadership Concepts

Bring forth the compelling case and emphasize this aspect of leadership to the leadership team. Why introduce these ideas? What is the burning platform obliging the response of building transformational leadership skills? Obviously, this is where you, the leader, take up the mantle of leading leaders.

Have Leaders Declare Individual Transformative Efforts

Moving from the abstract idea to concrete actions, each leader should select an area to experiment with and demonstrate the new leadership skills. Bold, creative leadership accomplished with an expanded view of community is the charge. As the coach, your participation in choosing a breakthrough results area is recommended. Like the area you chose for yourself, what results area would create a dramatic jump in overall organizational outcomes when preformed by the leader?

Coach Your Leaders on Mind-Sets

Know that a key value you bring to the coaching relationship is helping leaders become conscious of their mind-sets. First, develop a common language and holistic set of performance mind-sets. From this stand, aid leaders in becoming reflective of their mind-sets. Understand that having the leader become reflective of mind-sets is different than you pointing out their mind-sets. Your role provides less impact if it is limited to being a critical spectator. Coaching is the process of aiding the leader in the reflective process.

Hold Leaders Accountable for Selected, Step-Function Results

Leadership performance will be, in the end, the product of the individual leader. Therefore, your coaching of leaders is to help in their skill acquisition, not to lead in the absence of their development. Your leverage area is holding the leaders accountable for results. And in the arena of transformational leadership, the results need to be step-function, breakthrough in nature.

Having leaders successfully take up the challenge of transformational leadership can be very invigorating, an energy-producing project in itself. Prior to undertaking such an initiative, focus on the expected outcomes and the manner in which you will measure both progress and the endpoint. See the challenge as an area to demonstrate your transformational leadership.

MOVING FORWARD

In the end, success in transforming your organization will be a function of fruitful action, not intellectual understanding. The intellect can help the action to be fruitful, but it cannot serve as a substitute. Having gained some knowledge in transformational leadership, the way forward is to put your ideas into action. Some actions will generate fruit, and others will result in rework. However, only through the application of ideas will you know— and learn. John Kotter had an insight into the value of practicing transformational leadership skills:

Leaders invest tremendous talent, energy, and caring in their change efforts, yet few see the results they had hoped for. But there is a good reason why so few organizations have transformed themselves. Today's leaders simply don't have much practice at large-scale change. Thirty years ago few organizations were thinking about radical reinvention, so there is little practical experience to be passed on to a new generation of managers. The good news is the percentages are bound to improve. The kinds of changes routinely undertaken by today's organizations—producing ever better products, more quickly, at ever lower cost—were unimaginable 30 years ago. Over the next decade, thousands of leaders will guide equally remarkable changes. That is more than a safe prediction; it is a social and economic necessity. All institutions need effective leadership, but nowhere is the need greater than in the organization seeking to transform itself.[2]

The need is clear, the case compelling. What is required is someone to lead your organization to transform itself in order to ensure survival. Will you do it?

SUMMARY LEARNINGS

1. Train transformational leadership, but more importantly, put concepts into practice, creating internalized learnings and skills.

2. Skill evaluations can be helpful if they are sought after by the leader and supported with multiple observations.

TO ACTION

1. Can you construct a personalized plan to seize transformational leadership skills? Select audacious performance goals in a key results area and apply bold leadership measures.

2. Are you able to select critical leaders within your organization, present the transformational leadership model, and establish areas for experimentation with the approach?

3. How can you hold leaders accountable for breakthrough results?

4. Can you act? Fruitful action by transformational leaders will transform your organization. Intellect only serves as an aid informing the action.

ENDNOTES

1. Idalene F. Kesner, "Leadership Development: Perk or Priority?" *Harvard Business Review* 81, no. 5 (2003): 29.
2. John P. Kotter, "Winning at Change," *Leader to Leader* 10 (1998): 27–33.

Appendix A
The Life Plan

WHAT IS A LIFE PLAN?

The life plan is both a document and a process that connects our daily activities with our deeper understanding of what gives meaning to our lives. Creating a life plan helps us define our personal goals and aspirations: what we want to create of ourselves and in the world around us.

WHY CREATE A LIFE PLAN?

There is a great deal of power in having both a personal vision and a clear picture of your current reality. Having this perspective will generate a force within you that will move you toward your vision, and the production of tangible results.

WHEREVER YOU ARE, START THERE

It has been our experience that people often hesitate to take the first step in developing a life plan. One reason is that many people believe that the document must be perfect and complete. Quite the opposite is intended. The life plan is a lifelong working document. Begin with an imperfect first version, knowing that you will enhance it over time. The key is to start.

REVISITING THE LIFE PLAN

The life plan is intended to be a living document. We suggest you revisit your life plan about once every year, and perhaps more frequently in times of personal change. Many people prefer to reexamine their life plan near their birthdays.

This life planning tool is divided into three parts:

I. The conceptual image document

II. The life plan

III. Monthly follow-up on progress

PART I—THE CONCEPTUAL IMAGE DOCUMENT

This document is designed for you, the individual. It consists of four general areas containing thought-provoking questions. It is not an evaluation tool; it is an individual improvement tool. You can respond to a question in answer form or in descriptive paragraphs. It is intended to spark introspection, consciousness, and personal direction setting. Your conceptual image document is dynamic. Consider your first draft to be version 1.0, to be periodically updated as you progress through life.

1. Conceptual image of yourself, both personal and professional

   - Who are you?

     - What do you do? Who do you do it with? What value do you add to your customers? To your organization? To the world?

     - How do you introduce yourself? Who do you say you are to others?

   - What are your personal strengths? Why? What are your technical and professional competencies?

   - What are your weaknesses? Why?

   - What do you have passion for? What gives you joy?

   - Who do you learn from? What are you learning from them? Are you a mentor to anyone? If so, to whom, and concerning what area?

   - How well do you manage the agreements you make with others and yourself? How do you manage trust with others? How trustworthy are you?

   - What are your core values? What operating principles for daily living have you derived from these values?

   - What results are you producing? Why? How do you achieve results? What is your approach when results are not forthcoming?

2. Purpose, personal, and professional vision

   - What is your life's purpose? Why are you here?

- If your life were on tape, and you fast-forwarded the tape so that you were at the end looking back, what do you see? How do you feel?

- What in your past would you change?

3. Goals and objectives (2–5 years), both personal and professional

   - What are your goals and objectives?

   - What areas in your life do these goals and objectives encompass? What areas are not addressed?

   - How would you know if these goals and objectives were accomplished?

4. Near-term actions (3–6 months)

   - What actions will you take to improve yourself personally and professionally? What results do you expect to create in the next 3–6 months?

     - To fulfill your life's purpose?

     - To move toward your vision?

     - To move toward your goals and objectives?

   - What will you experiment with? What risks will you take?

   - What will you . . .

     - Read?

     - Do?

     - Study?

     - Experience?

   - What feedback will you seek?

   - What relationships will you create, mend, or improve?

   - How will you build agreements and trust?

PART II—LIFE PLAN

Significant Life Events

A significant life event is a specific happening, a critical incident, a key episode in your past, set in a particular time and place. It is a specific moment in your life that stands out to you for some reason. Describe several of the most critical incidents in your life to date. What was the impact of these events on the course of your life and who you are as a person?

_____

_____

_____

_____

_____

_____

_____

_____

_____

_____

_____

_____

_____

_____

_____

_____

_____

_____

_____

_____

_____

_____

_____

_____

Life Purpose

What is your purpose for being? If you already defined your life's purpose in your conceptual image document (CID), simply reflect on what you wrote as part of the preparation for creating your life plan.

_____

_____

_____

_____

_____

_____

_____

_____

_____

_____

_____

_____

_____

_____

_____

_____

_____

_____

_____

_____

_____

_____

_____

Values and Principles

Core values need no rationale or external justification, nor do they sway with trends and fads of the day. Principles are self-evident guidelines for human conduct, basic truths. What are your personal core values? Which principles are most important to you? What values and principles do you live by?

_____

_____

_____

_____

_____

_____

_____

_____

_____

_____

_____

_____

_____

_____

_____

_____

_____

_____

_____

_____

_____

_____

_____

_____

_____

Five-Year Vision

When you fast-forward your life's videotape five years ahead, what do you see? Who are you and how are you engaged in life? If you developed a five-year image in your CID, simply reflect on what you wrote as part of the preparation for creating your life plan.

_____

_____

_____

_____

_____

_____

_____

_____

_____

_____

_____

_____

_____

_____

_____

_____

_____

_____

_____

_____

_____

_____

_____

Planning the Parts of the Whole

In this section, seven areas of life are offered. However, other areas can be added or substituted in order to better fit how you categorize your life's major areas. Within each area, you are asked to describe a future vision (or point of arrival), a current state (or point of departure), and the actions required to achieve your vision. For each area in which you want to focus, establish one or more specific, measurable goals and outline your current performance related to these goals.

As you complete this section, don't feel pressured to sign up for aggressive goals in each area. While it can be appealing and seductive to set aggressive goals, try to focus on what is realistic for you. Most of us have experienced disappointment in the area of goal setting—unmet New Year's resolutions is a common example. Our suggestion is to focus your goals on three to five areas. Consider the option of merely maintaining and monitoring other areas in which you've chosen not to focus.

If you are struggling with which projects to take on, please stop for a minute and review your prior work. Reread your life's purpose, your principles, your values, and so on. Trust these core areas to guide you in this planning process.

Vocational

Point of Arrival (result you choose to create on the vocational horizon)

Point of Departure (results you are currently creating on the vocational horizon)

Actions Required/Milestones

    1. Specific Measurable Goals:

       Current Results:

    2. Specific Measurable Goals:

       Current Results:

    3. Specific Measurable Goals:

       Current Results:

Intellectual

Point of Arrival (result you choose to create on the intellectual horizon)

Point of Departure (results you are currently creating on the intellectual horizon)

Actions Required/Milestones

1. Specific Measurable Goals:

   Current Results:

2. Specific Measurable Goals:

   Current Results:

3. Specific Measurable Goals:

   Current Results:

Family

Point of Arrival (result you choose to create on the family horizon)

Point of Departure (results you are currently creating on the family horizon)

Actions Required/Milestones

1. Specific Measurable Goals:

   Current Results:

2. Specific Measurable Goals:

   Current Results:

3. Specific Measurable Goals:

   Current Results:

Financial

Point of Arrival (result you choose to create on the financial horizon)

Point of Departure (results you are currently creating on the
financial horizon)

Actions Required/Milestones

1. Specific Measurable Goals:

   Current Results:

2. Specific Measurable Goals:

   Current Results:

3. Specific Measurable Goals:

   Current Results:

Community

Point of Arrival (result you choose to create on the community horizon)

Point of Departure (results you are currently creating on the
community horizon)

Actions Required/Milestones

1. Specific Measurable Goals:

   Current Results:

2. Specific Measurable Goals:

   Current Results:

3. Specific Measurable Goals:

   Current Results:

Spiritual

Point of Arrival (result you choose to create on the spiritual horizon)

Point of Departure (results you are currently creating on the spiritual horizon)

Actions Required/Milestones

    1. Specific Measurable Goals:

       Current Results:

    2. Specific Measurable Goals:

       Current Results:

    3. Specific Measurable Goals:

       Current Results:

Physical

Point of Arrival (result you choose to create on the physical horizon)

Point of Departure (results you are currently creating on the physical horizon)

Actions Required/Milestones

    1. Specific Measurable Goals:

       Current Results:

    2. Specific Measurable Goals:

       Current Results:

    3. Specific Measurable Goals:

       Current Results:

PART III—MONTHLY FOLLOW-UP OPPORTUNITIES FOR SELF-REFLECTION

To reinforce the personal work that you have done so far, we recommend that you schedule self-reflection time once a month (a half hour to an hour). You can complete the following monthly exercises over the course of the coming year at whatever pace feels appropriate.

Month 1

What is the legacy you would like to have in your organization or in the world? In other words, what would you like to be known for?

_____

_____

_____

_____

_____

_____

_____

_____

_____

_____

_____

_____

_____

_____

_____

_____

_____

_____

_____

_____

Month 2

Write down or reflect upon an example of when you were on-purpose this month. What did it feel like? Write down or reflect upon an example of when you were off-purpose. What did it feel like? What did you do or not do to get yourself back on track?

_____

_____

_____

_____

_____

_____

_____

_____

_____

_____

_____

_____

_____

_____

_____

_____

_____

_____

_____

_____

_____

_____

_____

_____

Month 3

Write about or reflect upon an experience this month that gave you joy. What was it? Who was involved? What about it was joyful for you? What does that tell you about yourself?

_____

_____

_____

_____

_____

_____

_____

_____

_____

_____

_____

_____

_____

_____

_____

_____

_____

_____

_____

_____

_____

_____

_____

Month 4

Reflect back on your leadership assessment. What progress, if any, have you made with respect to your opportunities for improvement? Why or why not? What risks will you take in the coming weeks and months to increase your personal effectiveness?

_____

_____

_____

_____

_____

_____

_____

_____

_____

_____

_____

_____

_____

_____

_____

_____

_____

_____

_____

_____

_____

Month 5

Think about someone you know, or have observed, that you admire and consider to be a great leader (formal or informal). What attributes do they possess and why are they admirable? Consider sharing with them what you admire and the impact they have had on you.

_____

_____

_____

_____

_____

_____

_____

_____

_____

_____

_____

_____

_____

_____

_____

_____

_____

_____

_____

_____

_____

_____

_____

_____

Month 6

Review your life plan and the results you indicated that you intend to produce in key aspects of your life. Where are you on track? Where are you off track? What midcourse adjustments, if any, will you make?

_____

_____

_____

_____

_____

_____

_____

_____

_____

_____

_____

_____

_____

_____

_____

_____

_____

_____

_____

_____

_____

Month 7

Write about or reflect upon an example this month of when you played or felt playful. What impact, if any, did it have on your level of energy and effectiveness? If you haven't built play into your day, start doing so. Use your imagination!

_____

_____

_____

_____

_____

_____

_____

_____

_____

_____

_____

_____

_____

_____

_____

_____

_____

_____

_____

_____

_____

_____

_____

Month 8

Write down or reflect upon an example of when you were on-purpose this month or these past few months. What did it feel like? Write down or reflect upon an example of when you were off-purpose. What did it feel like? What did you do, or not do, to get yourself back on track?

_____

_____

_____

_____

_____

_____

_____

_____

_____

_____

_____

_____

_____

_____

_____

_____

_____

_____

_____

_____

_____

_____

_____

Month 9

Write about or reflect upon your connection to your organization's change efforts. What results are you producing? Why or why not?

_____

_____

_____

_____

_____

_____

_____

_____

_____

_____

_____

_____

_____

_____

_____

_____

_____

_____

_____

_____

_____

_____

_____

Month 10

Reflect on a time in the last month or so when you felt energized. What happened? Who was involved? Why was the experience energizing? What does that tell you about yourself?

_____

_____

_____

_____

_____

_____

_____

_____

_____

_____

_____

_____

_____

_____

_____

_____

_____

_____

_____

_____

_____

_____

_____

Month 11

Reflect back on your leadership assessment. What progress, if any, have you made with respect to your opportunities for improvement? Why or why not? What risks will you take in the coming weeks and months to increase your personal effectiveness?

_____

_____

_____

_____

_____

_____

_____

_____

_____

_____

_____

_____

_____

_____

_____

_____

_____

_____

_____

_____

_____

_____

_____

Month 12

Sit down with your life plan and review the results you have created over the course of the last year. What did you accomplish? Why did you produce the results you did? Why did you not produce some results you wanted to? Create version 2.0 of your life plan.

_____

_____

_____

_____

_____

_____

_____

_____

_____

_____

_____

_____

_____

_____

_____

_____

_____

_____

_____

_____

_____

_____

Appendix B

Transformational Leadership Assessment Survey

The following survey can be used to assess your skills in transformational leadership. After completing the survey, a scoring tool is provided.

In the following survey, you will answer questions about yourself in three settings. The first setting asks you about how you individually like to work. The second setting asks you about how you like to work on teams. The third setting asks you how you like to work on major projects. Using a scale of 1–7, please answer the following questions as honestly as you possibly can:

1   That doesn't describe me at all

2

3   That describes me occasionally

4

5   That describes me a lot of the time

6

7   That describes me all of the time

Note that few people will have all 7s or all 1s

_____   1.   Because of my skills, I am usually picked to be on major projects.

_____   2.   Because of my skills, I enjoy working on complicated, difficult issues.

_____ 3. Because of my skills, people often want me on their team.

_____ 4. I am not nervous with having others responsible for my rewards.

_____ 5. I am successful because I focus on the details.

_____ 6. I derive my energy from a clear sense of personal purpose, vision, and goals.

_____ 7. I enjoy achieving goals.

_____ 8. I enjoy creating novel solutions to routine problems.

_____ 9. I enjoy making goals.

_____ 10. I enjoy making sure details are taken care of.

_____ 11. I enjoy problem solving.

_____ 12. I enjoy putting together diverse people to formulate teams.

_____ 13. I enjoy solving complex problems.

_____ 14. I enjoy the day-to-day tasks of keeping major projects on schedule.

_____ 15. I enjoy working in a team to solve difficult problems.

_____ 16. I enjoy working in an orderly fashion where goals and objectives are clear.

_____ 17. I enjoy working long hours if I know it will lead to the desired output.

_____ 18. I enjoy working problems where there are *known* solutions.

_____ 19. I enjoy working with others on a project.

_____ 20. I get frustrated when people want to go against the rational process.

_____ 21. I hate doing the same thing over and over.

_____ 22. I need to know how what I do fits into the big picture.

_____ 23. I possess an abundance of energy.

_____ 24. I think it is important for the people on the project to bond as a group.

_____ 25. I think there is a logical answer to all problems.

_____ 26. I try to help others get their work done.

_____ 27. I understand how to get work done within the organization.

_____ 28. I would rather do different things every day than do the same thing every day.

_____ 29. In a team setting, I am often the one that takes the notes.

_____ 30. In a team setting, I am the one that always asks "Why are we doing this?"

_____ 31. In a team setting, I am the one that usually solves problems.

_____ 32. In a team setting, I am the one that usually takes on most of the work.

_____ 33. In a team setting, I enjoy brainstorming new ideas.

_____ 34. In a team setting, I enjoy coming up with novel solutions to routine problems.

_____ 35. In a team setting, I enjoy writing the vision statement for our team.

_____ 36. In a team setting, I hate doing the same thing over and over.

_____ 37. In a team setting, I make sure everyone understands how the work fits in toward the organization's vision.

_____ 38. In a team setting, I make sure our solutions are rational and practical.

_____ 39. In a team setting, I make sure we understand the goal of the team.

_____ 40. In a team setting, I see my role as motivating others to do their task.

_____ 41. In a team setting, I work harder when I know that others want to achieve the same goals that I do.

_____ 42. In a team setting, I work with others to make sure deadlines are met.

_____ 43. In a team setting, I would prefer that everyone has separate duties.

_____ 44. In a team setting, I would rather have the group I work with be happy and achieve okay results than have the group be unhappy and achieve outstanding results.

_____ 45. In a team setting, people look to me to help find solutions.

_____ 46. In a team setting, people would describe me as being good at scheduling.

_____ 47. In a team setting, when I am finished with my work, I try to help others.

_____ 48. In my organization, I communicate the importance of the project to others who are working on the project.

_____ 49. In my organization, I start project meetings by reviewing the vision of the project.

_____ 50. In my organization, I work best when I have a close connection with the people I am working with.

_____ 51. In my relationship with other people, I tap my own energy to build excitement in others about a project.

_____ 52. In my relationships, I consistently seek clarity of roles and responsibilities for moving a project ahead.

_____ 53. In my relationships with other people, people would describe me as the energetic catalyst.

_____ 54. People depend on me to do what I say I will.

_____ 55. People frequently come to me when they have a question about how to make something happen within the organization.

_____ 56. People would describe me as a loner.

_____ 57. People would describe me as analytical.

_____ 58. People would describe me as being good at time management.

_____ 59. People would describe me as capable and hardworking.

_____ 60. People would describe me as compassionate.

_____ 61. People would describe me as creative.

_____ 62. People would describe me as goal-oriented.

_____ 63. People would describe me as kind.

_____ 64. People would describe me as someone who is grounded in the current reality.

_____ 65. People would describe me as supportive.

_____ 66. People would describe me as tenacious.

_____ 67. Understanding why I am doing a project helps me to do better.

_____ 68. When I lead a team meeting, I have an agenda.

_____ 69. Who I do the work with is as important as the work I do.

_____ 70. When working on a major project, I am the one asking "Why are we here?"

_____ 71. When working on a major project, I enjoy brainstorming new ways to implement and execute the project.

_____ 72. When working on a major project, I keep a tight schedule of who is doing what.

_____ 73. When working on a major project, I look for people being put on the project that have similar goals.

_____ 74. When working on a major project, I make sure everybody's contributing toward the overall goal.

_____ 75. When working on a major project, I make sure everybody's making unique contributions.

_____ 76. When working on a major project, I make sure roles are clear.

_____ 77. When working on a major project, I make sure that people understand how the project is connected to their personal goals.

_____ 78. When working on a major project, I think there is one best process (or solution).

_____ 79. When working on a major project, I try to find alignment between individual needs and the organizational needs.

_____ 80. When working on a major project, I work with others until we are all complete.

_____ 81. When working on a major project, people look to me to come up with unique ideas.

_____ 82. When working on a major project, people often ask my advice on how to proceed.

_____ 83. With regard to my organization, I consistently strive to meet or exceed the organization's goals.

_____ 84. With regard to my organization, I focus on the organization's vision when exploring problem-solving options.

_____ 85. With regard to my organization, I have established measurable goals for performance.

_____ 86. With regard to my organization, I link individual performance goals to the overall business goals.

_____ 87. With regard to my organization, I utilize the core values of the organization to define the boundaries for solving a problem.

_____ 88. With regard to the organization, I recruit people to work on projects based on their personal interests and energy.

INSTRUCTIONS FOR SCORING THE SELF-ASSESSMENT

Each question in the self-assessment corresponds with one of the eight characteristics of transformational leadership. The questions corresponding with each transformational leadership characteristic are as follows:

Administrative (14 questions)
   5, 10, 14, 16, 27, 29, 46, 52, 55, 58, 64, 68, 72, 76

Analytical (12 questions)
   11, 18, 20, 25, 31, 38, 45, 57, 78, 82, 84, 87

Performer (13 questions)
   1, 2, 3, 7, 13, 15, 32, 43, 54, 59, 83, 85, 86

Energetic (8 questions)
   6, 17, 23, 42, 51, 53, 66, 80

Empowering (10 questions)
   4, 19, 26, 37, 40, 47, 74, 77, 79, 88

Creative (10 questions)
   8, 21, 28, 33, 34, 36, 61, 71, 75, 81

Visionary (10 questions)
9, 22, 30, 35, 39, 48, 49, 62, 67, 70

Community-Builder (11 questions)
12, 24, 41, 44, 50, 56, 60, 63, 65, 69, 73

For each characteristic, total your responses (1–7) for each question and then divide your total by the number of questions for that characteristic. For example, if the total response for the administrative characteristic is 70, divide 70 by the total number questions for that characteristic. For the administrative characteristic, the total is 14 questions. In this example, the average score for the administrative area is 5 on a scale of 1–7. Those characteristics with the highest average score would be considered your strengths. Those with the lowest average score would be your learning opportunities. Consider what action you might take in at least two of the learning opportunity areas and develop a personal improvement plan.

Appendix C

Summary Lesson Plans on Each Major Model in the Book

WHAT IS TRANSFORMATION?

Generally, there are three change focuses within organizations and they are often confused. The first is standardization. Standardization involves decreasing variation, having a system become more predictable. A majority of people within an organization focus upon the operating system, and can find ample opportunities to tighten the execution of systems and deliver a reduction of variation.

By contrast, continuous improvement efforts are aimed at achieving gradual, positive changes in performance. In a statistical sense, standardization is about reducing variation, while improvement is about shifting the mean.

Breakthrough improvement or transformation is yet a third kind of change within an organization (see Figure C.1). It is typically the role of the top leadership team to lead breakthrough change. The complete definition of organizational transformation is *the marked change in the nature or function of organizational systems creating discontinuous, step-function improvement in sought-after result areas.*

This definition requires both the discernment of the change generating the transformation and the ensuing performance results. The results are a consequence of the system changes. Differing from reduction of variation or continuous improvement, step-function improvement constitutes a dramatic and pointed shift in results. Also referred to as breakthrough improvement, a conspicuous shift in results is its hallmark. It can be seen on a control chart as a discontinuous break with past results, a step up in performance, or a break from the previous system results. For transformation to be declared, the results are categorized as step-function or breakthrough improvement.

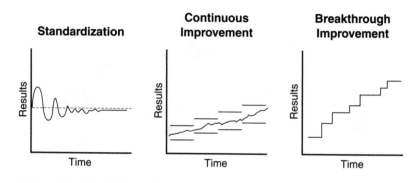

Figure C.1   Change focuses.

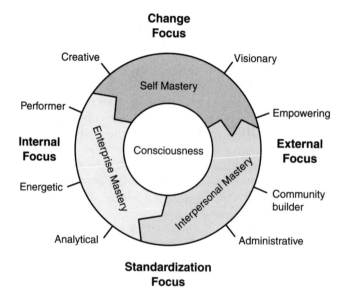

Figure C.2   Transformational leadership.

Transformational leadership is the comprehensive and integrated leadership capacities required of individuals, groups, or organizations to produce transformation as evidenced by step-functional improvement (see Figure C.2).

This leadership approach, in particular, was designed to be integrated and holistic, serving as a powerful framework to anchor your own ideas and experiments in leadership. Without this kind of comprehensive framework, leaders are at risk of continually adopting the latest leadership style-of-the-day found in the local airport bookstore. While new approaches can be insightful, holding a comprehensive, integrated view of leadership gives you a Christmas tree, so to speak, on which to hang the latest ornament.

Through our leadership readings and experiences in working with organizations to produce transformation, we have discerned that a new kind of leadership is required. At the heart of transformational leadership is consciousness of self and the ability to raise consciousness in others.

Transformational leaders must also hold an internal and external focus, seeking to understand the internal dynamics of the organization while simultaneously attending to external forces and a broader community of people holding the organization's license to live. Understanding the value of standardization and change to the organization and the tension that can arise between the two is also a requirement of the transformational leader.

Transformational leadership transcends either/or thinking and requires the leader to embody both leadership and management talent.

LEADING A LIFE OF MEANING

Human beings have unlimited potential to create lives of accomplishment and personal fulfillment. However, a great number of people wonder where they are going in life. It may be human nature to ask, "Why am I here?" But to put forth an answer is often the courageous step not taken. What purpose does my existence serve? What difference can I make with my life? Answering these questions is not an easy task. Creating a life of meaning requires patience, commitment, and time dedicated to personal mastery (see Figure C.3).

You can see the power and results of others who have achieved clarity of life purpose. Through the works of well-known and influential leaders, such as Dr. Martin Luther King Jr. and Nelson Mandela, and the achievements of ordinary people, you can see the power that clarity of purpose holds in your life. Remarkable results can be achieved by conscious and purposeful people working to forward the goals of an organization. As a transformational leader, a first step in creating a purposeful organization is to personally build a life of meaning. Clarity of life purpose, values, and direction in life are imperative to deliberate and productive growth.

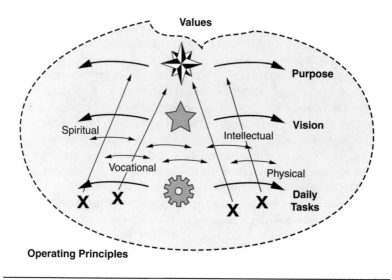

Figure C.3   Leading a life of meaning.

PERFORMANCE MIND-SETS

Performance in work and other life domains is fundamentally shaped by a person's individual mind-set. For example, making excuses for failed performance traps one in a mind-set of pointing to mechanisms, events, or circumstances as something over which no one has control or power to change. Adopting an intentional mind-set states that you will make it through every barrier to produce the result, leading to bold action and opportunity for learning. In short, results are the sole source of your intentions, whether conscious or unconscious.

The five mind-sets that result in performance are intention, authenticity, abundance, oneness, and power beyond measure (see Figure C.4). For each performance mind-set, there is a polar mind-set that hinders performance.

In transformational leadership, your first job is to be able to see your own mind-set at work. Being able to see mind-sets at work in others is also a capacity of a transformational leader. The leader's top responsibility is to assist individuals in self-reflection. This is accomplished through coaching—using inquiry and observation methods without judgment.

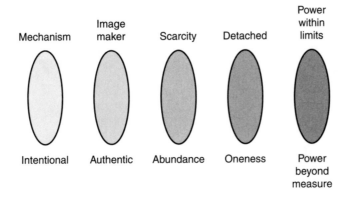

Figure C.4   Performance mind-sets.

About the Authors

Stephen Hacker is a managing partner of Transformation Systems International, LLC and a board member and former executive director of The Performance Center. Hacker has previously coauthored *The Trust Imperative: Performance Improvement through Productive Relationships* (ASQ Quality Press, 2002), and *Work Miracles* (Insight Press, 1999, second printing 2003). He is a sought-after international speaker and consultant, having aided in the transformation of many noted organizations. Prior to joining The Performance Center, he served as senior leader of several manufacturing/engineering organizations within Procter & Gamble. He has earned an MBA from the University of New Orleans and a BS in mechanical engineering from Tulane University.

Tammy Roberts is a managing partner of Transformation Systems International LLC and the president of The Performance Center. Roberts's diverse background includes working as the committee aide in the Ohio state legislature, associate director of public policy for the American Society of Internal Medicine and manager of government relations followed by manager of research and development for an international accrediting organization focused on establishing healthcare quality standards. She has seventeen years' experience working with governmental organizations and nonprofits around the country. Roberts earned her BA in interdisciplinary studies at Miami University in Oxford, Ohio.

Index